AMALFI COAST

Travel Guide 2024 - 2025

The Ultimate Resource for Itineraries, Transportation,
Where to Stay, What to See, Where to Eat, and Insider Tips

Sandi H. Newman

Disclaimer
The information contained in this book is for general informational purposes only. While the author has made every effort to ensure the accuracy and completeness of the information provided, we make no representations or warranties of any kind, express or implied, about the accuracy, reliability, suitability, or availability with respect to the book or the information, products, services, or related graphics contained in the book for any purpose. Any reliance you place on such information is therefore strictly at your own risk.

The author will not be liable for any false, inaccurate, inappropriate, or incomplete information presented in this book. The author will not be liable for any damages of any kind arising from the use of this book, including but not limited to direct, indirect, incidental, punitive, and consequential damages.

The author does not assume and hereby disclaims any liability to any party for any loss, damage, or disruption caused by errors or omissions, whether such errors or omissions result from negligence, accident, or any other cause.

All information is provided "as is" with no guarantee of completeness, accuracy, timeliness, or of the results obtained from the use of this information, and without warranty of any kind, express or implied, including, but not limited to warranties of performance, merchantability, and fitness for a particular purpose.

This book includes links to other websites for informational purposes only. These links do not signify an endorsement of the content or opinions contained within those websites. The author has no control over the nature, content, and availability of those sites.

Travel information such as visa requirements, transportation schedules, prices, and business operations are subject to change and may vary. It is recommended that travelers verify such information independently.

Any product names, logos, brands, and other trademarks or images featured or referred to within this book are the property of their respective trademark holders. These trademark holders are not affiliated with the author, and they do not sponsor or endorse this book.

The author reserves the right to make changes or updates to the content of this book at any time without prior notice.

By using this book, you agree to the terms of this disclaimer. If you do not agree with any part of this disclaimer, do not use this book.

TABLE OF CONTENTS

INTRODUCTION

This guide is your go-to resource for everything you need to know about this stunning region in Italy. Whether you are planning your first visit or you have been here before, you will find valuable information to help you make the most of your trip.

The Amalfi Coast is a 50-kilometer stretch of coastline along the southern edge of Italy's Sorrentine Peninsula, in the Campania region. It is famous for its dramatic cliffs, crystal-clear waters, and charming towns that seem to cling precariously to the steep mountainsides. Each town has its unique charm and story, creating a mosaic of different cultures and histories that make the coast a fascinating destination.

The history of the Amalfi Coast is as rich and varied as its landscape. In ancient times, the region was inhabited by Roman aristocrats who built luxurious villas along the coastline. During the Middle Ages, Amalfi became a powerful maritime republic, playing a key role in trade between the Mediterranean and the Orient. The historical significance of the area is evident in its architecture, art, and cultural traditions. As you walk through the narrow streets of towns like Amalfi, Positano, and Ravello, you can feel the echoes of the past and see the remnants of ancient times in the buildings and monuments.

The towns of the Amalfi Coast each offer something special. Positano is known for its steep, narrow streets lined with colorful houses and its beautiful beach, Spiaggia Grande. Amalfi, the town that gives the coast its name, boasts a stunning cathedral with an impressive facade. Ravello, perched high above the sea, is famous for its breathtaking views and beautiful gardens like Villa Cimbrone and Villa Rufolo. Praiano offers a quieter alternative to the more touristy towns, with lovely beaches and a relaxed atmosphere. Minori and Maiori are known for their wide beaches and delicious local cuisine, while Atrani, one of the smallest towns in Italy, is a hidden gem with a picturesque square and charming streets.

The natural beauty of the Amalfi Coast is one of its main attractions. The coastline is dotted with stunning beaches, hidden coves, and clear waters perfect for swimming, snorkeling, and other water activities. The dramatic cliffs and lush greenery provide a beautiful backdrop for outdoor adventures such as hiking and biking. One of the most famous hiking trails in the region is the Path of the Gods, which offers spectacular views of the coastline and is a must-do for nature lovers.

Experiencing the local culture is another highlight of visiting the Amalfi Coast. The region hosts numerous festivals and events throughout the year, celebrating everything from local saints to the bounty of the sea. Music lovers will enjoy the Ravello Festival, a renowned classical music festival held in the stunning gardens of Villa Rufolo. Local markets are a great way to experience the culture and pick up unique souvenirs. You will find everything from handmade ceramics to locally produced limoncello, a lemon liqueur that is a specialty of the region. Don't miss the opportunity to try the local cuisine, which features fresh seafood, locally grown produce, and delicious pastries.

Planning a trip to the Amalfi Coast can seem daunting, but this guide will make it easy. We will cover everything from visa requirements and travel insurance to the best ways to get around. Whether you prefer to travel by bus, boat, or car, we will provide tips to help you navigate the region with ease. Accommodation options on the Amalfi Coast are varied, catering to all budgets and preferences. From luxury hotels and charming bed and breakfasts to budget-friendly hostels and family-run guesthouses, there is something for everyone. We will help you find the perfect place to stay, whether you are looking for a romantic getaway, a family vacation, or a solo adventure.

The Amalfi Coast offers something for everyone, whether you are traveling alone, with a partner, or with family. Solo travelers will find plenty of opportunities for adventure and relaxation, from exploring hidden coves to enjoying a quiet meal in a local trattoria. Couples can enjoy romantic walks, sunset cruises, and intimate dinners with stunning views. Families will appreciate the many child-friendly attractions and activities, from sandy beaches to interactive museums.

Day trips to nearby islands like Capri and Ischia, as well as visits to the ancient ruins of Pompeii and Herculaneum, are popular excursions from the Amalfi Coast. We will provide detailed itineraries and tips for making the most of these excursions. Your safety and well-being are important, and we will provide all the information you need to stay healthy and safe during your trip. From emergency contacts and local healthcare facilities to tips for staying safe while exploring, you will be well-prepared for any situation.

The Amalfi Coast is a place that stays with you long after you have left. Its beauty, history, and culture create a unique and unforgettable experience. Whether you are lounging on the beach, exploring ancient ruins, or savoring a delicious meal, every moment spent on the Amalfi Coast is special. This guide is your key to unlocking the secrets of this incredible region and making the most of your visit. Enjoy the journey and create memories that will last a lifetime.

CHAPTER 1

THE HISTORY AND CULTURE OF AMALFI COAST

The Amalfi Coast, with its picturesque towns and dramatic landscapes, is a region rich in history and culture that has developed over centuries. This coastal area, stretching along the southern edge of Italy's Sorrentine Peninsula, is a fascinating tapestry of human and natural history. To understand the Amalfi Coast, one must dig into its ancient origins, its rise as a maritime power, and its enduring cultural legacy.

The history of the Amalfi Coast begins in ancient times. The area was originally inhabited by indigenous Italic tribes, who lived in small villages scattered along the rugged coastline. However, it was the arrival of the Romans that began to shape the region's historical trajectory. The Romans, recognizing the strategic and aesthetic value of the coast, established a number of settlements here. Wealthy Roman aristocrats built grand villas along the coastline, taking advantage of the stunning views and the mild climate. These villas were not only luxurious residences but also centers of social and political life.

After the fall of the Roman Empire, the region experienced a period of turmoil and change. The decline of Roman authority left a power vacuum that was filled by various groups, including the Byzantines and the Lombards. It was during this time that Amalfi began to emerge as a significant power. By the 9th century, Amalfi had become an independent maritime republic. This period marked the beginning of Amalfi's golden age. As a maritime republic, Amalfi was one of the first in Italy, predating the more famous maritime republics of Venice and Genoa. The city's strategic location along major trade routes allowed it to become a bustling center of commerce.

Amalfi's sailors and merchants were renowned for their skills and daring. They established trade routes that stretched across the Mediterranean, reaching as far as the Middle East and North Africa. Amalfi merchants traded in spices, precious metals, textiles, and other valuable goods, making the city incredibly wealthy. The Amalfitans also developed advanced navigational techniques and created one of the earliest maritime codes, known as the "Tabula Amalphitana," which influenced maritime law for centuries.

The prosperity of the Amalfi Coast during this period is evident in the architectural and cultural achievements of the time. The most iconic structure from this era is the Amalfi Cathedral, dedicated to Saint Andrew, the patron saint of Amalfi. This cathedral, with its striking Arab-Norman style, reflects the diverse influences that shaped the region. The intricate mosaics and the imposing bell tower are testaments to the wealth and artistic sophistication of Amalfi during its peak.

Despite its success, the Republic of Amalfi could not maintain its dominance forever. By the 12th century, Amalfi's power began to wane due to a combination of natural disasters, such as earthquakes and tsunamis, and the rise of rival maritime republics like Pisa and Genoa. In 1137, Amalfi was conquered by the Normans, marking the end of its independence. Although it never regained its former glory as a maritime power, Amalfi remained an important cultural and economic center.

The subsequent centuries saw the Amalfi Coast becoming part of the Kingdom of Naples and experiencing the influences of various ruling dynasties. During the Renaissance, the region became a hub for artists, writers, and scholars, attracted by its natural beauty and inspiring landscapes. The towns along the coast continued to thrive, with agriculture, fishing, and trade forming the backbone of the local economy.

In modern times, the Amalfi Coast has transformed into one of Italy's most popular tourist destinations. The same natural beauty and cultural richness that captivated ancient Romans and Renaissance artists now draw visitors from around the world. Tourism has become the primary industry, with the region's historic sites, stunning views, and charming towns providing the perfect backdrop for a memorable vacation.

Culturally, the Amalfi Coast is a treasure trove of traditions and customs that have been preserved and passed down through generations. Festivals and celebrations play a significant role in the life of the local communities. One of the most famous is the Feast of Saint Andrew in Amalfi, which includes a dramatic procession and fireworks. Each town has its own unique festivities, often linked to religious events or local history, providing a glimpse into the area's rich cultural heritage.

The cuisine of the Amalfi Coast is another important aspect of its cultural identity. The region's fertile land and access to the sea have resulted in a culinary tradition that emphasizes fresh, local ingredients. Lemons, known as "sfusato amalfitano," are a symbol of the region and are used in a variety of dishes and drinks, including the famous limoncello liqueur. Seafood is a staple of the local diet, with dishes like spaghetti alle vongole (spaghetti with clams) and fresh fish grilled to perfection. The influence of centuries of trade is evident in the use of spices and ingredients that originated far from the Amalfi Coast but have become integral to its cuisine.

The Amalfi Coast's history and culture are as captivating as its stunning landscapes. From its origins as a haven for Roman aristocrats to its rise as a powerful maritime republic, and its transformation into a modern tourist paradise, the region's story is one of resilience, creativity, and enduring charm. The cultural richness of the Amalfi Coast is reflected in its architecture, festivals, and culinary traditions, making it a destination that offers both beauty and depth to those who visit. This guide aims to provide you with a comprehensive understanding of this remarkable region, helping you to appreciate its past and present as you explore its many wonders.

Climate and Best Time to Visit

The Amalfi Coast, located along the southern edge of Italy's Sorrentine Peninsula, is renowned for its stunning landscapes, charming towns, and rich history. One of the key factors that make the Amalfi Coast a beloved destination for travelers worldwide is its pleasant climate. Understanding the climate and the best time to visit this beautiful region can greatly enhance your travel experience, allowing you to make the most of your trip.

The Amalfi Coast enjoys a Mediterranean climate, characterized by mild, wet winters and hot, dry summers. This type of climate is typical of coastal areas in southern Italy and is one of the reasons why the region is so attractive to visitors. The weather is generally favorable throughout the year, but there are distinct differences between the seasons that can influence the best time to visit based on your preferences and activities.

Winter on the Amalfi Coast, which lasts from December to February, is generally mild compared to other parts of

Europe. Temperatures during this season range from 8°C (46°F) to 14°C (57°F). While it is not as cold as many other destinations, winter is the wettest season on the Amalfi Coast. Rainfall is frequent, and the skies are often overcast. However, if you enjoy a quieter atmosphere and don't mind the occasional rain shower, visiting during the winter can be quite rewarding. The tourist crowds are at their lowest, and you can explore the towns and landmarks without the usual hustle and bustle. Additionally, accommodation prices are significantly lower, making it an ideal time for budget-conscious travelers.

Spring, which spans from March to May, is one of the best times to visit the Amalfi Coast. The weather during this season is delightful, with temperatures gradually warming up from 12°C (54°F) to 22°C (72°F) by May. The rainfall decreases, and the days become longer and sunnier. Spring is a wonderful time to experience the natural beauty of the region. The hills and terraces are covered in vibrant wildflowers, and the famous lemon trees of the Amalfi Coast begin to bloom, filling the air with a fragrant scent. Spring is also the beginning of the tourist season, but it is not as crowded as the summer months. This makes it an excellent time for sightseeing, hiking, and enjoying outdoor activities without the intense heat or large crowds.

Summer, from June to August, is the peak tourist season on the Amalfi Coast. The weather is hot and dry, with temperatures ranging from 24°C (75°F) to 30°C (86°F) or higher in July and August. The sea temperatures are perfect for swimming, making it the ideal time for beach lovers. However, the popularity of the Amalfi Coast during summer means that it can get quite crowded, especially in popular towns like Positano and Amalfi. Prices for accommodations and services are at their highest, and it is advisable to book well in advance if you plan to visit during this period. Despite the crowds and higher costs, summer offers a lively and vibrant atmosphere with numerous festivals, events, and activities taking place. It is a great time to experience the cultural richness of the region, enjoy boat trips along the coast, and savor the delicious local cuisine at open-air restaurants.

Autumn, which lasts from September to November, is another excellent time to visit the Amalfi Coast. The weather remains warm and pleasant in September and early October, with temperatures ranging from 20°C (68°F) to 26°C (79°F). As the season progresses, temperatures gradually cool down, reaching around 15°C (59°F) in November. Autumn is a wonderful time to explore the region's natural beauty and historic sites. The summer crowds begin to dwindle, providing a more relaxed and enjoyable experience. The sea remains warm enough for swimming in early autumn, and the hiking trails are less crowded, making it a great time for outdoor activities. The vineyards and orchards are in full harvest, and you can enjoy the local produce, including grapes, figs, and chestnuts. Autumn also brings several local festivals and events, offering a glimpse into the rich cultural traditions of the Amalfi Coast.

When planning your visit to the Amalfi Coast, it is important to consider your preferences and the type of experience you are seeking. Each season offers a unique charm and different opportunities for exploration and enjoyment. Whether you prefer the lively atmosphere of summer, the blooming beauty of spring, the mild and colorful autumn, or the quiet serenity of winter, the Amalfi Coast has something to offer all year round.

To make the most of your trip, it is advisable to plan ahead and book accommodations and activities in advance, especially if you are visiting during the peak summer months. Additionally, packing appropriately for the season will ensure you are comfortable and prepared for the weather conditions. Light, breathable clothing and sunscreen are essential for the summer, while layers and a good raincoat will be useful in the cooler, wetter months.

The Amalfi Coast's climate is one of its many appealing features, offering a pleasant and enjoyable environment for visitors throughout the year. By understanding the seasonal variations and planning your visit accordingly, you can experience the best that this beautiful region has to offer. Whether you are drawn by the warm summer sun, the colorful spring blossoms, the mild autumn days, or the peaceful winter atmosphere, the Amalfi Coast is a destination that promises unforgettable memories and a truly enriching travel experience.

Travel Tips and Etiquette

Traveling to the Amalfi Coast is a delightful experience, filled with stunning scenery, delicious food, and a rich cultural heritage. To make the most of your visit, it's important to be aware of some travel tips and etiquette that will help you navigate this beautiful region smoothly and respectfully.

First and foremost, understanding the local customs and etiquette can go a long way in making your trip more enjoyable. Italians are known for their warmth and hospitality, but like any culture, they have their own set of social norms. Greeting people with a friendly "Buongiorno" (good morning) or "Buonasera" (good evening) is a simple way to show respect. When entering shops, restaurants, or even when meeting people on the street, these greetings are appreciated and help set a positive tone for your interactions. When dining out, remember that meal times in Italy are a bit different from those in other countries. Lunch is usually served between 1:00 PM and 3:00 PM, and dinner starts around 8:00 PM and can go on until late. It's not uncommon for restaurants to close between lunch and dinner service, so plan your meals accordingly. Tipping is not mandatory in Italy, as a service charge is often included in the bill. However, leaving a small tip for good service is always appreciated. A few coins or rounding up the bill is usually sufficient.

Public transportation is a convenient way to get around the Amalfi Coast. Buses and ferries connect the main towns and offer breathtaking views along the way. When using public transport, it's important to validate your ticket before boarding. Validation machines are typically located at the entrance of buses and ferries. Failure to validate your ticket can result in a fine. Also, try to be patient and polite, as buses can get crowded, especially during peak tourist season.

Driving in the Amalfi Coast can be both thrilling and challenging. The roads are narrow and winding, often with steep drops on one side. If you choose to rent a car, be prepared for tight turns and limited parking. It's essential to drive carefully and be mindful of local driving habits. Italians tend to drive assertively, so staying alert and cautious is crucial. Additionally, parking can be scarce and expensive in popular towns like Positano and Amalfi, so consider using public transport or parking outside the town centers and walking in.

Walking is one of the best ways to explore the Amalfi Coast, allowing you to discover hidden gems and enjoy the scenery at your own pace. Comfortable shoes are a must, as the terrain can be steep and uneven. Many towns have stairs instead of streets, and exploring on foot will often involve climbing and descending many steps. Staying hydrated and taking breaks will help you manage the physical demands of walking around these beautiful but challenging landscapes. Respecting the local environment is important for preserving the natural beauty of the Amalfi Coast. Dispose of your trash properly and recycle when possible. Avoid littering and be mindful of your environmental footprint. The region is home to many protected areas and delicate ecosystems, so staying on marked trails and not disturbing wildlife is essential.

Language can be a barrier for some travelers, but making an effort to learn a few basic Italian phrases can greatly enhance your experience. While many locals in tourist areas speak some English, they will appreciate your attempts to communicate in their language. Simple phrases like "Per favore" (please), "Grazie" (thank you), and "Mi scusi" (excuse me) can go a long way in fostering goodwill.

Shopping in local markets and stores can be a wonderful experience. The Amalfi Coast is known for its beautiful ceramics, handmade sandals, and local food products like limoncello and olive oil. Bargaining is not common practice in Italy, so it's best to accept the listed price or make a polite inquiry if you are purchasing multiple items. Supporting local artisans and businesses not only helps the local economy but also allows you to take home unique and meaningful souvenirs.

When visiting churches and other religious sites, dress modestly out of respect. This means covering your shoulders and knees. Many churches provide shawls or coverings for visitors who are not appropriately dressed, but it's a good idea to bring your own. Being quiet and respectful during your visit will ensure a pleasant experience for everyone.

The pace of life on the Amalfi Coast is generally slower and more relaxed than in many other parts of the world. Embrace this laid-back attitude by taking the time to savor your meals, enjoy leisurely walks, and engage in conversations with locals. Rushing through your itinerary will only detract from the experience. Instead, allow yourself to fully immerse in the beauty and culture of the region.

Finally, be prepared for the unexpected. Travel plans can change due to weather conditions, especially in coastal areas. Ferries might be canceled, or roads might be closed due to landslides. Having a flexible itinerary and backup plans will help you manage any surprises. Travel insurance is also a good idea to cover any unforeseen events.

Visiting the Amalfi Coast can be a truly unforgettable experience if you approach it with respect and a willingness to embrace the local customs and pace of life. By following these travel tips and etiquette guidelines, you can ensure a smooth and enjoyable journey, filled with wonderful memories and enriching experiences. Whether you are strolling through the narrow streets of Positano, savoring a meal in Amalfi, or hiking the Path of the Gods, being mindful of these tips will help you get the most out of your visit to this beautiful part of Italy.

CHAPTER 2

PLANNING YOUR TRIP

Visa Requirements

Visiting the Amalfi Coast, like traveling to any foreign destination, involves understanding the visa requirements that apply to your nationality. Italy is a member of the Schengen Agreement, which means that the visa regulations for entering the Amalfi Coast are the same as for the rest of the Schengen Area. This agreement includes most European Union countries and a few non-EU members, allowing for border-free travel within the region for short stays.

For many travelers, particularly those from countries that have agreements with the Schengen Zone, a visa may not be necessary for short stays. Citizens of the United States, Canada, Australia, New Zealand, Japan, South Korea, and many other countries do not need a visa for stays of up to 90 days within a 180-day period. This period applies to travel for tourism, business, family visits, or attending cultural or sports events. It's important to note that this 90-day limit applies to the entire Schengen Area, not just Italy. So, if you plan to travel to other Schengen countries as well, your total time in all these countries cannot exceed 90 days within a 180-day period.

However, even if you do not need a visa, there are still some requirements you must meet. Firstly, your passport must be valid for at least three months beyond your planned date of departure from the Schengen Area. It is also advisable to have at least two blank pages in your passport. You should be able to provide proof of sufficient funds to cover your stay, a return or onward ticket, and travel insurance that covers medical expenses and emergencies during your trip.

For those who do require a visa, the process involves applying for a Schengen visa. This visa allows you to travel within the entire Schengen Area for up to 90 days within a 180-day period. The application process typically requires submitting a completed application form, your passport, a recent passport-sized photo, proof of travel insurance, evidence of accommodation bookings, a detailed travel itinerary, and proof of sufficient financial means to support yourself during your stay.

You will also need to provide a cover letter stating the purpose of your visit and outlining your travel plans. If you are visiting friends or family, a letter of invitation from your host in Italy, along with a copy of their ID or residence permit, may be required. For business travelers, an invitation letter from the company you will be visiting and a letter from your employer are necessary. The application process also includes a visa fee, which varies depending on your nationality and the specifics of your trip.

It's crucial to apply for your visa well in advance of your planned travel dates. The processing time for a Schengen visa can take up to 15 calendar days, but it can be longer during peak travel times or if additional documentation is required. Some nationalities may also have to attend an interview at the consulate or embassy.

Once you have your visa, make sure to understand the conditions attached to it. The Schengen visa allows you to move freely within the Schengen Area, but you must comply with the duration of stay and purpose of visit as specified in your visa. Overstaying your visa or using it for purposes other than what it was issued for can lead to penalties, including being banned from entering the Schengen Area in the future.

For longer stays, such as for study, work, or family reunification, different types of visas and permits are required. These typically involve more extensive application processes and documentation. For example, if you plan to study in Italy, you will need a student visa, which requires proof of enrollment in an Italian educational institution, proof of accommodation, and evidence of sufficient financial resources. Similarly, for work visas, you will need a job offer from an Italian employer and authorization from the Italian government.

It's always a good idea to check the latest visa requirements and regulations on the official website of the Italian embassy or consulate in your country before making any travel arrangements. Visa regulations can change, and it's important to have the most current information. Additionally, some travelers may benefit from consulting with a visa service or immigration lawyer to ensure that all requirements are met and to facilitate the application process.

Understanding the visa requirements for visiting the Amalfi Coast is a crucial part of travel planning. Whether you need a visa or not, being prepared with the right documents and knowledge will help ensure a smooth and enjoyable trip. The beauty and charm of the Amalfi Coast are well worth the effort, and with the right preparation, you can fully enjoy all that this stunning region has to offer.

Health and Safety Tips

Traveling to the Amalfi Coast is an incredible experience, filled with beautiful landscapes, charming towns, and rich culture. To ensure that your visit is both enjoyable and safe, it is important to be aware of some health and safety tips. These tips will help you stay healthy, avoid common hazards, and have a smooth and memorable trip.

First and foremost, it is essential to have travel insurance that covers medical expenses. While Italy has a good healthcare system, unexpected medical issues can arise, and having insurance will ensure you receive the care you need without incurring significant costs. Make sure your travel insurance covers not only medical emergencies but also trip cancellations, lost luggage, and other potential disruptions.

Before you travel, check if you need any vaccinations. Generally, there are no special vaccinations required for Italy, but it is always good to ensure that your routine vaccinations, such as measles, mumps, rubella, diphtheria, tetanus, and pertussis, are up to date. If you have any chronic health conditions or specific health concerns, consult your doctor before traveling.

While on the Amalfi Coast, staying hydrated is crucial, especially during the hot summer months. The coastal climate can be quite warm, and it is easy to become dehydrated while exploring the picturesque towns and hiking the scenic trails. Carry a reusable water bottle and drink plenty of water throughout the day. Tap water in Italy is generally safe to drink, but if you prefer, you can also buy bottled water.

Sun protection is another important aspect to consider. The sun can be very strong, particularly in the summer, so it is essential to protect your skin from sunburn. Use a high-SPF sunscreen, wear a hat, and use sunglasses to protect your eyes. It is also a good idea to wear light, breathable clothing that covers your skin, especially during the peak sun hours between 10 AM and 4 PM.

When it comes to food and water safety, the Amalfi Coast is known for its delicious cuisine, and you will want to try the local specialties. However, to avoid any stomach issues, make sure to eat at reputable restaurants and food stalls. The seafood is fresh and delicious, but ensure it is well-cooked. If you have food allergies, it is wise to learn the Italian names for the ingredients you need to avoid and communicate your needs clearly to restaurant staff.

The Amalfi Coast is famous for its steep terrain and narrow, winding roads. While this adds to its charm, it can also pose some safety challenges. If you are driving, be cautious and drive slowly, especially around curves and in narrow areas. Italian drivers can be fast and assertive, so stay alert. If you are not comfortable driving in these conditions, consider using public transportation or hiring a local driver.

Walking is one of the best ways to explore the towns of the Amalfi Coast, but be prepared for a lot of stairs and uneven paths. Wear comfortable, sturdy shoes with good grip to navigate the steep streets and steps. Take your time and be cautious, especially if the paths are wet or crowded. If you have mobility issues, it is important to plan your itinerary carefully, as some areas may be difficult to access.

Safety in public areas is generally good on the Amalfi Coast, but it is always wise to be cautious. Petty crime, such as pickpocketing, can occur, particularly in crowded tourist spots. Keep your valuables secure and be mindful of your surroundings. Use a money belt or a secure bag to carry your important documents, money, and other valuables. Avoid displaying expensive items like jewelry and electronics openly.

In case of emergencies, it is useful to know the local emergency numbers. In Italy, the emergency number for police, fire, and medical assistance is 112. Familiarize yourself with the location of the nearest hospital or medical facility to your accommodation. Most towns on the Amalfi Coast have pharmacies, which can provide basic medical supplies and advice for minor health issues.

If you plan on swimming or participating in water activities, be aware of the sea conditions. The waters around the Amalfi Coast are generally safe for swimming, but currents can be strong in some areas. Pay attention to local warnings and flags at beaches, which indicate whether it is safe to swim. It is also a good idea to swim in designated areas where lifeguards are present.

Hiking is a popular activity on the Amalfi Coast, with many trails offering spectacular views. If you plan to hike, choose trails that match your fitness level and experience. The Path of the Gods is one of the most famous hikes, but it can be challenging, with steep sections and uneven terrain. Wear appropriate footwear, carry enough water, and bring a map or GPS device. It is also advisable to hike with a companion and let someone know your plans before you set out.

Being mindful of the local culture and customs is part of staying safe and respecting the community. Italians are generally warm and welcoming, but it is important to be respectful of their traditions. Dress modestly when visiting churches and religious sites, and be aware that some places may require shoulders and knees to be covered. Using polite greetings and basic Italian phrases can go a long way in creating positive interactions with locals.

Finally, be flexible and patient. Travel can sometimes come with unexpected delays or changes in plans, especially in a region known for its leisurely pace of life. Allow yourself extra time for getting around, and don't be too rigid with your schedule. Embracing the relaxed atmosphere of the Amalfi Coast will help you have a more enjoyable and stress-free experience.

Visiting the Amalfi Coast can be a wonderful and safe experience if you take the necessary health and safety precautions. By staying hydrated, protecting yourself from the sun, being cautious with food and water, navigating the terrain carefully, and respecting local customs, you can ensure that your trip is both enjoyable and safe. Whether you are soaking in the views, exploring the charming towns, or indulging in the local cuisine, these tips will help you make the most of your visit to this beautiful part of Italy.

Currency and Budgeting

Visiting the Amalfi Coast, one of Italy's most beautiful destinations, requires careful planning, especially when it comes to understanding the currency and managing your budget. Knowing how to handle your finances during your trip will help you enjoy everything this stunning region has to offer without any unexpected surprises.

The currency used in Italy, including the Amalfi Coast, is the Euro (EUR). It is important to familiarize yourself with the current exchange rate before you travel, as this will help you budget your expenses and understand the value of what you are spending. You can check the exchange rate online or at your bank before you leave. Having a rough idea of how much things cost in euros compared to your home currency will help you manage your money more effectively.

When it comes to accessing money, there are several options available. ATMs are widely available throughout the Amalfi Coast, and they are a convenient way to withdraw euros. Using ATMs linked to your bank or credit union often provides better exchange rates than currency exchange offices. However, it is important to inform your bank of your travel plans to avoid any issues with your card being blocked for suspicious activity. Additionally, check with your bank regarding any fees for international withdrawals, as these can add up quickly.

Credit and debit cards are widely accepted in most hotels, restaurants, and shops along the Amalfi Coast. Visa and Mastercard are the most commonly accepted cards, but it is always a good idea to carry some cash for smaller establishments, local markets, or situations where cards may not be accepted. When using your card, choose to be charged in euros rather than your home currency to avoid dynamic currency conversion fees, which can be more expensive.

Budgeting for your trip to the Amalfi Coast depends on your travel style and preferences. Accommodation is one of the biggest expenses. The Amalfi Coast offers a range of options, from luxury hotels and villas to more budget-friendly guesthouses and hostels. If you plan to stay in popular towns like Positano or Amalfi, be prepared for higher prices, especially during the peak tourist season. Booking your accommodation well in advance can help you secure better rates and more options.

Eating out on the Amalfi Coast can also vary in cost. Fine dining restaurants with spectacular views can be quite expensive, while local trattorias, pizzerias, and cafés offer more affordable options without compromising on the quality of food. Trying local specialties, such as fresh seafood, pasta dishes, and pastries, is a highlight of visiting the region. To save money, consider having a larger meal at lunchtime when many restaurants offer fixed-price menus, known as "menu del giorno," which are often better value than the evening à la carte options.

Transportation is another factor to consider in your budget. Public transportation, such as buses and ferries, is a cost-effective way to travel between towns on the Amalfi Coast. The SITA bus network connects most of the major towns and is relatively inexpensive. Ferries offer a scenic and enjoyable way to travel along the coast, but they can be more expensive than buses. If you prefer the convenience of a rental car, keep in mind the additional costs of fuel, parking, and potential tolls. Parking can be particularly challenging and costly in popular towns, so factor this into your budget if you choose to drive.

Activities and sightseeing are an essential part of any trip to the Amalfi Coast. Entrance fees to historical sites, museums, and gardens can add up, so plan accordingly. Some attractions, like the Amalfi Cathedral or the gardens of Villa Rufolo in Ravello, charge an admission fee, while others, such as exploring the charming streets of Positano or hiking the Path of the Gods, are free. Researching and prioritizing the activities that interest you most will help you allocate your budget effectively.

Shopping is another area where you might want to spend money. The Amalfi Coast is known for its beautiful ceramics, handmade sandals, and local food products like limoncello and olive oil. While it is tempting to buy many souvenirs, setting a shopping budget can help you manage your spending. Look for local markets and smaller shops for unique and often more affordable items compared to tourist-heavy areas.

Tipping in Italy is not as customary as it is in some other countries, but it is appreciated for good service. In restaurants, a service charge (servizio) is often included in the bill. If it is not, leaving a small tip of around 10% is sufficient. For other services, such as hotel staff or taxi drivers, rounding up the fare or leaving a small tip is a nice gesture but not obligatory.

To manage your budget effectively, consider using a travel app or keeping a daily record of your expenses. This will help you stay on track and avoid overspending. Breaking down your budget into categories such as accommodation, food, transportation, activities, and shopping will give you a clear picture of where your money is going and help you make adjustments if needed.

Understanding the currency and budgeting for your trip to the Amalfi Coast is crucial for a smooth and enjoyable experience. By familiarizing yourself with the euro, planning your expenses, and being mindful of your spending, you can fully enjoy the beauty and charm of this incredible region without any financial stress. Whether you are dining at a seaside restaurant, exploring historical sites, or simply soaking in the stunning views, a well-managed budget will help you make the most of your visit to the Amalfi Coast.

Packing List: Essentials for Your Trip

Packing for a trip to the Amalfi Coast requires thoughtful planning to ensure you have everything you need for a comfortable and enjoyable visit. This stunning region of Italy, with its picturesque towns, beautiful beaches, and rich history, offers a variety of activities and experiences. To make the most of your trip, it is essential to pack appropriately for the climate, terrain, and activities you plan to enjoy. Here is a detailed guide to help you prepare your packing list.

First and foremost, consider the time of year you will be visiting. The Amalfi Coast experiences a Mediterranean climate with hot, dry summers and mild, wet winters. If you are visiting during the summer months, you will need light, breathable clothing to stay cool in the heat. Think cotton dresses, linen shirts, shorts, and skirts. It is also a good idea to bring a wide-brimmed hat and sunglasses to protect yourself from the strong sun. Sunscreen with a high SPF is a must to prevent sunburn, especially if you plan to spend time at the beach or exploring outdoors.

For spring and autumn visits, the weather can be more variable. Pack layers that you can add or remove as needed. A lightweight jacket or sweater is useful for cooler evenings or unexpected chilly days. Long-sleeved shirts, jeans, and comfortable pants will keep you comfortable during these seasons. Don't forget to bring a compact umbrella or a waterproof jacket, as rain is more common during these times of the year.

If you are traveling in winter, the weather is generally mild, but it can be cool and wet. Pack warmer clothing such as sweaters, long pants, and a medium-weight coat. A scarf and gloves might also be useful for particularly chilly days. Although it rarely snows, the coastal breeze can make it feel colder than it actually is.

Footwear is another important consideration. The Amalfi Coast's towns are known for their steep, narrow streets and many stairs. Comfortable walking shoes with good grip are essential for navigating the uneven terrain. Sneakers or sturdy sandals are a good choice for daytime exploring. If you plan to hike the famous trails, such as the Path of the Gods, consider bringing hiking shoes or boots. For evenings out, pack a pair of nicer shoes, but make sure they are still comfortable enough for walking.

Beachwear is a must if you plan to enjoy the stunning beaches along the Amalfi Coast. Bring a couple of swimsuits, as well as a cover-up or sarong for when you are not in the water. A beach bag, flip-flops, and a quick-drying towel are also essential. Many beaches in the region are rocky rather than sandy, so water shoes can be helpful for protecting your feet.

When it comes to accessories, a small backpack or daypack is ideal for carrying your essentials while you explore. This can include items like a water bottle, snacks, sunscreen, a map, and a camera. A crossbody bag or a money belt can keep your valuables secure and easily accessible. If you plan to visit religious sites, bring a scarf or shawl to cover your shoulders as a sign of respect.

Toiletries and personal care items are another important aspect of your packing list. While you can buy most things in Italy, it is easier to bring your own essentials. Pack travel-sized versions of your toiletries to save space. This should include items like shampoo, conditioner, soap, toothpaste, and a toothbrush. Don't forget any prescription medications you may need, along with a copy of the prescription in case you need a refill. A basic first aid kit with band-aids, antiseptic wipes, and any over-the-counter medications you might need, such as pain relievers or motion sickness tablets, is also a good idea.

Electronics are a part of modern travel, and you will want to ensure you have everything you need to stay connected and capture your memories. Bring a smartphone with a good camera, as well as a charger and an international plug adapter. If you plan to use your phone for navigation or translation, consider downloading offline maps and language apps before you leave. A portable power bank can be handy for keeping your devices charged while you are out and about. If you are a photography enthusiast, bring a camera with extra batteries and memory cards.

Documents and money are critical items for any trip. Make sure you have your passport, along with any necessary visas. It is a good idea to bring photocopies of your passport and other important documents, such as travel insurance information and reservation confirmations, in case you lose the originals. Carry some euros in cash for small purchases, as well as a credit or debit card for larger expenses. Notify your bank of your travel plans to avoid any issues with card transactions while you are abroad.

Finally, consider any special items that might enhance your trip. A good book or an e-reader can be great for relaxing on the beach or during downtime. If you enjoy writing or drawing, a journal or sketchbook can be a wonderful way to capture your experiences. Binoculars can enhance your enjoyment of the stunning vistas and local wildlife. If you have space, a small travel guidebook can be helpful for learning more about the places you visit.

Packing for a trip to the Amalfi Coast requires a thoughtful approach to ensure you have everything you need for a comfortable and enjoyable experience. By considering the climate, activities, and specific needs of your trip, you can create a comprehensive packing list that covers all the essentials. From clothing and footwear to toiletries and electronics, being well-prepared will help you make the most of your visit to this beautiful part of Italy. Whether you are strolling through the charming towns, hiking the scenic trails, or relaxing on the beach, having the right items with you will ensure a smooth and memorable journey.

CHAPTER 3

GETTING THERE AND AROUND

International and Domestic Flights

When planning a trip to the Amalfi Coast, understanding the details about international and domestic flights is crucial for a smooth and enjoyable journey. This beautiful region in southern Italy is well-connected by air, with several options available depending on your starting point and travel preferences.

For international travelers, the primary gateway to the Amalfi Coast is Naples International Airport, also known as Capodichino Airport (NAP). Naples Airport is the closest major airport to the Amalfi Coast, located approximately 60 kilometers (about 37 miles) from the town of Amalfi. It serves many international and domestic flights, making it a convenient entry point.

If you are flying from outside Europe, you will likely need to connect through one of Europe's major hub airports before arriving in Naples. Airports such as Rome Fiumicino (FCO), Milan Malpensa (MXP), Frankfurt (FRA), Paris Charles de Gaulle (CDG), and London Heathrow (LHR) offer frequent flights to Naples. These hubs have extensive international connections, making it easy to find a suitable flight.

Booking your flights well in advance can help you secure better fares and more convenient flight times. Use flight comparison websites to search for the best deals and consider setting up fare alerts to monitor price changes. Flexible travel dates can also help you find lower prices, as flight costs can vary significantly depending on the time of year and day of the week.

Upon arrival at Naples International Airport, you have several options for reaching the Amalfi Coast. One of the most convenient ways is to hire a private transfer or taxi, which can take you directly to your accommodation. This option offers the most comfort and convenience, especially if you have a lot of luggage or are traveling with family. Alternatively, you can take a bus from the airport to Sorrento, and from there, connect to local buses or ferries to reach your destination on the coast.

For those considering domestic flights within Italy, Naples International Airport is well-connected to other major Italian cities. If you are flying from Rome, Milan, Venice, or other cities, there are frequent flights to Naples. Domestic flights are generally quick and efficient, making it easy to incorporate a visit to the Amalfi Coast into a broader Italian itinerary.

Another option for reaching the Amalfi Coast is to fly into Rome Fiumicino Airport, Italy's largest and busiest airport. Rome is approximately 270 kilometers (about 167 miles) from the Amalfi Coast, and while it is further than Naples, it offers more international flight options and can be a good alternative, especially if you plan to explore other parts of Italy as well. From Rome, you can take a train to Naples, which takes about 1 to 2 hours on the high-speed trains. Once in Naples, you can follow the same options for reaching the coast.

Milan Malpensa Airport is another major international gateway. While it is much further from the Amalfi Coast, at around 800 kilometers (about 497 miles), it can be an option if you find a significantly better flight deal or plan to explore northern Italy. From Milan, you can take a domestic flight to Naples or a high-speed train to Rome and then continue to Naples and the Amalfi Coast.

When choosing your flights, consider the total travel time, including layovers and connections. While it might be tempting to choose the cheapest flight, longer layovers and multiple connections can make your journey more tiring. Direct flights or those with shorter layovers are generally more convenient, even if they are slightly more expensive.

In addition to commercial flights, there are also some budget airlines that operate within Europe, offering low-cost flights to Naples. Airlines such as Ryanair, EasyJet, and Wizz Air often have lower fares compared to traditional carriers. However, be aware that budget airlines may charge extra for checked luggage, seat selection, and other services. It is important to read the fine print and understand the total cost before booking.

Traveling with children or elderly family members may require additional considerations. Ensure you have all necessary travel documents, including passports and any required visas. Pack snacks, entertainment, and any necessary medications in your carry-on bag to keep everyone comfortable during the flight. Arriving at the airport with plenty of time before your flight can help reduce stress and allow you to handle any unexpected issues that may arise.

When planning your trip, it is also worth considering travel insurance that covers flight cancellations, delays, and lost luggage. This can provide peace of mind and financial protection in case of any travel disruptions.

Planning your flights to the Amalfi Coast involves several key considerations. Whether you are flying internationally or domestically, Naples International Airport is the most convenient gateway, with alternative options available through Rome and Milan. Booking in advance, choosing the best flight connections, and preparing for your journey can ensure a smooth and enjoyable start to your visit to this stunning region. By understanding the flight options and making informed choices, you can focus on enjoying the beauty and charm of the Amalfi Coast once you arrive.

Transportation Options: Trains, Buses, and Ferries

When visiting the Amalfi Coast, one of the most important aspects of planning your trip is understanding the various transportation options available to get around this beautiful region. The Amalfi Coast is known for its stunning cliffs, picturesque towns, and narrow, winding roads, making transportation a crucial part of your travel experience.

The Amalfi Coast is not directly served by a train line, but trains are still a key part of getting to and from the region. The nearest major train station is in Salerno, which is well-connected to other parts of Italy. If you are coming from Rome, Naples, or other major cities, you can take a high-speed train to Salerno. Trenitalia and Italo are the main train operators in Italy, offering frequent and reliable services. From Rome, the journey to Salerno takes about two hours on a high-speed train, while from Naples, it is just around 30 to 40 minutes.

Once you arrive in Salerno, you will need to switch to another mode of transportation to reach the Amalfi Coast. One popular option is to take a bus. The SITA bus company operates a network of buses that connect Salerno with various towns along the coast, including Amalfi, Positano, and Ravello. The buses are a cost-effective and convenient way to travel, offering stunning views of the coastline along the way. However, be prepared for potentially crowded conditions, especially during peak tourist season. It is advisable to check the bus schedules in advance and arrive at the bus stop early to secure a seat.

Another option for reaching the Amalfi Coast from Salerno is by ferry. Ferries are a scenic and enjoyable way to travel, providing a unique perspective of the coastline from the water. Several ferry companies operate services between Salerno and the coastal towns, including Travelmar and NLG. The ferry ride is relatively quick, taking around 35 to 70 minutes depending on your destination. Ferries are generally less crowded than buses and offer a more relaxed and comfortable journey, making them a great choice if you prefer a leisurely travel experience.

Once you are on the Amalfi Coast, getting around between towns can also be done by bus or ferry. The SITA bus network covers the entire coast, making it easy to hop between towns. Buses run regularly, but it is important to be aware that the narrow and winding roads can result in delays, especially during busy times. Despite this, buses remain one of the most affordable ways to travel around the coast. Tickets can be purchased at local tobacco shops (tabacchi) or directly from the driver, though it is cheaper to buy them in advance.

Ferries are another excellent option for traveling between coastal towns. They operate between key destinations like Amalfi, Positano, and Sorrento, offering a scenic and efficient way to move around. During the summer months, additional services are often added to accommodate the higher number of tourists. Ferry schedules can vary, so it is important to check the timetables in advance and plan your journey accordingly. While ferries are generally more expensive than buses, the breathtaking views and comfortable ride make them well worth the extra cost.

In addition to buses and ferries, private transportation options are available for those who prefer a more personalized travel experience. Taxis and private car services can be hired for direct transportation between towns or for guided tours of the region. While this is the most expensive option, it offers the highest level of convenience and comfort, especially if you are traveling with a group or have a lot of luggage.

Driving is another option for getting around the Amalfi Coast, but it comes with its own set of challenges. The roads are narrow, winding, and often congested, making driving a potentially stressful experience for those not used to such conditions. Parking can also be difficult to find and expensive, particularly in popular towns like Positano and Amalfi. If you do choose to drive, it is essential to be cautious and patient, and to consider parking outside the town centers and walking in to avoid the worst of the traffic and parking issues.

For those who enjoy a more active approach to travel, renting a scooter or bicycle can be a fun and flexible way to explore the Amalfi Coast. Scooters are a popular choice among locals and tourists alike, allowing you to navigate the narrow streets and find parking more easily than with a car. However, the same cautions apply: the roads can be challenging and require careful driving. Bicycles are another great option, particularly for shorter distances or if you want to explore specific areas at your own pace. E-bikes, which are available for rent in many towns, can help with the hilly terrain.

Walking is another viable option, especially within the towns themselves. The Amalfi Coast is known for its pedestrian-friendly streets, and many of the best sights can be explored on foot. Comfortable walking shoes are a must, as the terrain can be steep and uneven. Walking also allows you to fully appreciate the charm and beauty of the towns, with their narrow alleys, stairways, and picturesque views at every turn.

Lastly, consider the practical aspects of using public transportation. Always carry some cash with you, as smaller shops and ticket vendors may not accept credit cards. It is also a good idea to have a small backpack or bag for your daily essentials, such as water, snacks, sunscreen, and a hat. Being prepared will ensure you can travel comfortably and make the most of your time on the Amalfi Coast.

Getting around the Amalfi Coast involves a mix of transportation options, each with its own advantages and considerations. Whether you choose to travel by train, bus, ferry, car, scooter, bicycle, or on foot, understanding the logistics and planning ahead will help you have a smooth and enjoyable experience. The key is to be flexible and prepared, allowing you to fully enjoy the stunning scenery, charming towns, and rich culture that the Amalfi Coast has to offer.

Car Rentals and Driving Tips

Renting a car and driving along the Amalfi Coast can be an incredibly rewarding experience, offering the freedom to explore this stunning region at your own pace. However, it also comes with its own set of challenges and considerations. To ensure a smooth and enjoyable journey, it's essential to be well-prepared and informed about the car rental process and the driving conditions you can expect to encounter.

When it comes to renting a car, there are several options available. Major international car rental companies, such as Hertz, Avis, Europcar, and Budget, operate in Italy, offering a range of vehicles to suit different needs and budgets. Additionally, there are local rental agencies that may provide competitive rates and personalized service. It is advisable to book your rental car in advance, especially during peak tourist seasons, to ensure availability and secure the best rates.

To rent a car in Italy, you will need a valid driver's license from your home country. If your license is not in Italian or does not use the Roman alphabet, it is recommended to obtain an International Driving Permit (IDP), which serves as a translation of your license. Most car rental companies will require you to be at least 21 years old, and some may have additional age restrictions or surcharges for drivers under 25 or over 70. You will also need a credit card in the name of the primary driver to secure the rental.

When choosing a rental car, consider the size and type of vehicle that will best suit your needs. The roads along the Amalfi Coast are narrow and winding, and parking can be limited, so a smaller car is often more practical. Compact or subcompact cars are easier to maneuver and park, while still providing enough space for passengers and luggage. If you plan to explore off the beaten path or prefer a more comfortable ride, a mid-size car or SUV may be a better option, though it may be more challenging to navigate in tight spaces.

Once you have your rental car, it's important to familiarize yourself with the driving conditions and local traffic laws. The Amalfi Coast is famous for its scenic but challenging roads, which can be daunting for drivers not used to such conditions. The main road, the SS163, also known as the Amalfi Drive, runs along the coastline from Sorrento to Salerno and offers breathtaking views of the sea and cliffs.

However, it is also narrow, with sharp bends and steep drop-offs, requiring careful and attentive driving.

One of the key tips for driving on the Amalfi Coast is to take it slow and stay alert. The speed limits are generally low, around 30 to 50 kilometers per hour (about 18 to 31 miles per hour), and it is important to adhere to them. The roads are often busy with traffic, including local buses, delivery trucks, and tourist coaches, which can make passing difficult. Be patient and wait for safe opportunities to overtake slower vehicles. Use your horn to signal your presence when approaching blind corners, as this is a common practice in Italy to alert oncoming traffic.

Parking is another important consideration when driving on the Amalfi Coast. Finding a parking spot can be challenging, especially in popular towns like Positano and Amalfi. Many towns have designated parking areas or garages where you can leave your car for a fee. It is advisable to use these facilities rather than attempting to park on the narrow streets. Look for blue lines, which indicate paid parking zones, and purchase a parking ticket from a nearby machine or kiosk. White lines indicate free parking, while yellow lines are reserved for residents or special permits.

In addition to parking fees, be aware of ZTL (Zona Traffico Limitato) zones, which are restricted traffic areas found in many Italian towns and cities. These zones are designed to reduce congestion and pollution in historic centers, and only authorized vehicles are allowed to enter during certain hours. Entering a ZTL zone without permission can result in hefty fines. Always look for signs indicating ZTL zones and plan your route accordingly. If your accommodation is within a ZTL zone, ask your host or hotel for guidance on how to obtain access.

Fuel stations are readily available along the coast and in the surrounding areas, but it is a good idea to fill up your tank before heading out on longer drives, as some stretches of road may not have many fueling options. Most fuel stations accept credit cards, but it is wise to carry some cash as a backup. Fuel in Italy can be more expensive than in other countries, so factor this into your budget. Diesel (diesel) is often cheaper than unleaded petrol (benzina), and many rental cars in Italy run on diesel.

Navigating the roads of the Amalfi Coast can be easier with the help of a GPS or a reliable navigation app on your smartphone. These tools can provide real-time traffic updates, suggest alternative routes, and help you avoid getting lost. However, it is always a good idea to carry a physical map as a backup, in case you encounter areas with poor signal or battery issues.

Driving defensively is crucial on the Amalfi Coast. Be prepared for local drivers who may be more aggressive or take risks that you are not accustomed to. Keep a safe distance from the vehicle in front of you, and be extra cautious when approaching intersections and pedestrian crossings. Pay attention to road signs and markings, which may be different from those in your home country.

If you find the idea of driving on the Amalfi Coast too daunting, there are alternatives to consider. Hiring a private driver or using taxi services can provide a stress-free way to travel between towns and attractions. Many drivers are knowledgeable about the area and can offer valuable insights and recommendations. Additionally, organized tours can provide a comprehensive experience without the need to navigate the roads yourself.

Renting a car and driving along the Amalfi Coast can be a wonderful way to explore this beautiful region, offering the freedom to visit hidden gems and enjoy the scenic views at your own pace. By being well-prepared, choosing the right vehicle, and following these driving tips, you can ensure a safe and enjoyable journey. Whether you are marveling at the coastal vistas, exploring charming towns, or simply savoring the journey, driving the Amalfi Coast can be a highlight of your trip to Italy.

Public Transportation Guide

Getting around the Amalfi Coast using public transportation is a practical and enjoyable way to explore this stunning region. The area is well-served by a network of buses, ferries, and trains that connect the various towns and attractions. Understanding how to use these transportation options can help you make the most of your visit without the stress of driving on narrow, winding roads. This guide will provide detailed information on how to navigate the Amalfi Coast using public transportation.

The Amalfi Coast is not directly connected by train, but trains are still an important part of reaching the region. The nearest major train station is in Salerno, which is well-connected to other parts of Italy. If you are coming from Rome, Naples, or other major cities, you can take a high-speed train to Salerno. Trenitalia and Italo are the main train operators in Italy, offering frequent and reliable services. From Rome, the journey to Salerno takes about two hours on a high-speed train, while from Naples, it is just around 30 to 40 minutes.

Once you arrive in Salerno, you can switch to buses or ferries to reach the Amalfi Coast. The SITA bus company operates a comprehensive network of buses that connect Salerno with various towns along the coast, including Amalfi, Positano, and Ravello. Buses are a cost-effective and convenient way to travel, offering stunning views of the coastline along the way. However, be prepared for potentially crowded conditions, especially during peak tourist season. It is advisable to check the bus schedules in advance and arrive at the bus stop early to secure a seat.

Tickets for SITA buses can be purchased at local tobacco shops (tabacchi), newsstands, or directly from the driver, though it is cheaper to buy them in advance. Make sure to validate your ticket in the machine on the bus, as failure to do so can result in a fine. The buses run regularly, but the narrow and winding roads can lead to delays, especially during busy times. Despite this, buses remain one of the most affordable ways to travel around the coast.

Another option for reaching the Amalfi Coast from Salerno is by ferry. Ferries are a scenic and enjoyable way to travel, providing a unique perspective of the coastline from the water. Several ferry companies operate services between Salerno and the coastal towns, including Travelmar and NLG. The ferry ride is relatively quick, taking around 35 to 70 minutes depending on your destination. Ferries are generally less crowded than buses and offer a more relaxed and comfortable journey, making them a great choice if you prefer a leisurely travel experience.

Once you are on the Amalfi Coast, getting around between towns can also be done by bus or ferry. The SITA bus network covers the entire coast, making it easy to hop between towns. Buses run regularly, but it is important to be aware that the narrow and winding roads can result in delays, especially during busy times. Despite this, buses remain one of the most affordable ways to travel around the coast. Tickets can be purchased at local tobacco shops (tabacchi) or directly from the driver, though it is cheaper to buy them in advance.

Ferries are another excellent option for traveling between coastal towns. They operate between key destinations like Amalfi, Positano, and Sorrento, offering a scenic and efficient way to move around. During the summer months, additional services are often added to accommodate the higher number of tourists. Ferry schedules can vary, so it is important to check the timetables in advance and plan your journey accordingly. While ferries are generally more expensive than buses, the breathtaking views and comfortable ride make them well worth the extra cost.

In addition to buses and ferries, private transportation options are available for those who prefer a more personalized travel experience. Taxis and private car services can be hired for direct transportation between towns or for guided tours of the region. While this is the most expensive option, it offers the highest level of convenience and comfort, especially if you are traveling with a group or have a lot of luggage.

Driving is another option for getting around the Amalfi Coast, but it comes with its own set of challenges. The roads are narrow, winding, and often congested, making driving a potentially stressful experience for those not used to such conditions. Parking can also be difficult to find and expensive, particularly in popular towns like Positano and

Amalfi. If you do choose to drive, it is essential to be cautious and patient, and to consider parking outside the town centers and walking in to avoid the worst of the traffic and parking issues.

For those who enjoy a more active approach to travel, renting a scooter or bicycle can be a fun and flexible way to explore the Amalfi Coast. Scooters are a popular choice among locals and tourists alike, allowing you to navigate the narrow streets and find parking more easily than with a car. However, the same cautions apply: the roads can be challenging and require careful driving. Bicycles are another great option, particularly for shorter distances or if you want to explore specific areas at your own pace. E-bikes, which are available for rent in many towns, can help with the hilly terrain.

Walking is another viable option, especially within the towns themselves. The Amalfi Coast is known for its pedestrian-friendly streets, and many of the best sights can be explored on foot. Comfortable walking shoes are a must, as the terrain can be steep and uneven. Walking also allows you to fully appreciate the charm and beauty of the towns, with their narrow alleys, stairways, and picturesque views at every turn.

Lastly, consider the practical aspects of using public transportation. Always carry some cash with you, as smaller shops and ticket vendors may not accept credit cards. It is also a good idea to have a small backpack or bag for your daily essentials, such as water, snacks, sunscreen, and a hat. Being prepared will ensure you can travel comfortably and make the most of your time on the Amalfi Coast.

Getting around the Amalfi Coast involves a mix of transportation options, each with its own advantages and considerations. Whether you choose to travel by train, bus, ferry, car, scooter, bicycle, or on foot, understanding the logistics and planning ahead will help you have a smooth and enjoyable experience. The key is to be flexible and prepared, allowing you to fully enjoy the stunning scenery, charming towns, and rich culture that the Amalfi Coast has to offer.

CHAPTER 4

ACCOMMODATION OPTIONS

Luxury Hotels and Resorts

The Amalfi Coast is one of the most picturesque and luxurious travel destinations in the world. Known for its stunning coastal scenery, charming towns, and rich cultural heritage, it attracts tourists seeking both relaxation and adventure. For those looking to indulge in a truly opulent experience, the region offers a range of luxury hotels and resorts that provide the highest standards of comfort, service, and amenities.

One of the most famous luxury hotels on the Amalfi Coast is Le Sirenuse, located in the heart of Positano. This historic hotel, once a private residence, offers breathtaking views of the Mediterranean Sea and the colorful houses that cascade down the cliffs. Each room and suite is elegantly decorated with a blend of antique and contemporary furnishings, providing a sophisticated yet cozy ambiance. Guests can enjoy world-class dining at the hotel's Michelin-starred restaurant, La Sponda, where the cuisine highlights fresh, local ingredients. The hotel also features a beautiful swimming pool, a spa offering a range of treatments, and a private boat for excursions along the coast.

Another prestigious property is the Belmond Hotel Caruso in Ravello. Perched high on a cliff overlooking the sea, this former 11th-century palace offers a serene and luxurious retreat. The hotel's infinity pool is one of the most iconic spots on the Amalfi Coast, with stunning views that stretch to the horizon. The rooms and suites are spacious and beautifully appointed, featuring marble bathrooms and private terraces. The Belmond Hotel Caruso also boasts exquisite gardens, a top-tier restaurant serving Mediterranean cuisine, and a wellness center offering personalized treatments.

In Amalfi, the NH Collection Grand Hotel Convento di Amalfi is a standout choice. This five-star hotel is housed in a restored 13th-century monastery, offering a unique blend of historical charm and modern luxury. The hotel's location, perched on a cliff above the town, provides panoramic views of the coast. Guests can relax in the infinity pool, dine at the gourmet restaurant, and explore the hotel's ancient cloisters and beautiful gardens. The rooms and suites are stylishly decorated with contemporary furnishings and offer all the modern amenities one would expect from a luxury hotel.

For those seeking a more intimate and exclusive experience, the Monastero Santa Rosa Hotel & Spa in Conca dei Marini is an excellent choice. This boutique hotel, set in a converted 17th-century monastery, offers only 20 rooms and suites, each uniquely decorated and offering stunning sea views. The hotel's gardens are a highlight, featuring terraced levels with aromatic herbs and flowers, as well as a striking infinity pool. The spa at Monastero Santa Rosa is renowned for its holistic treatments, providing a tranquil sanctuary for relaxation and rejuvenation. The hotel's restaurant serves gourmet dishes inspired by traditional Italian cuisine, with an emphasis on fresh, local ingredients.

The Palazzo Avino, located in the medieval town of Ravello, is another top luxury hotel on the Amalfi Coast. This family-owned property, set in a 12th-century villa, combines historic charm with modern elegance. The rooms and suites are lavishly decorated, offering breathtaking views of the sea or the lush gardens. The hotel's Michelin-starred restaurant, Rossellinis, serves exceptional Italian cuisine, and guests can also enjoy casual dining at the Terrazza Belvedere. The Palazzo Avino features a stunning rooftop terrace, a spa with a range of treatments, and a private beach club in nearby Marmorata.

In Positano, Il San Pietro di Positano is a legendary luxury hotel that has been a favorite of discerning travelers for decades. Built into the cliffs, the hotel offers unparalleled views of the coastline and the Tyrrhenian Sea. The rooms and suites are beautifully appointed, each with a private terrace and elegant furnishings. The hotel's Michelin-starred restaurant, Zass, offers exquisite dining with a focus on locally sourced ingredients. Guests can relax on the private beach, take a dip in the sea-view pool, or enjoy a treatment at the spa. Il San Pietro also offers a range of activities, including cooking classes, boat excursions, and hiking tours.

For those who prefer a contemporary style, the Casa Angelina in Praiano is an excellent choice. This modern boutique hotel offers a sleek and minimalist design, with bright, airy rooms and stunning sea views. The hotel's rooftop terrace is a highlight, offering panoramic views of the coast and a perfect spot for enjoying a cocktail at sunset. Casa Angelina's restaurant serves gourmet Mediterranean cuisine, and the hotel's spa offers a range of treatments to help guests unwind. The hotel also provides direct access to a private beach, where guests can relax and soak up the sun.

In Maiori, the Hotel Botanico San Lazzaro offers a luxurious escape in a lush, botanical setting. The hotel's rooms and suites are elegantly decorated, each with a private balcony or terrace offering stunning views of the sea. The hotel's gardens are a highlight, featuring a wide variety of exotic plants and flowers. Guests can enjoy gourmet dining at the hotel's restaurant, relax by the outdoor pool, or indulge in a treatment at the spa. The hotel also offers a range of activities, including cooking classes, wine tastings, and guided tours of the local area.

Finally, the Villa Cimbrone in Ravello offers a truly unique and luxurious experience. This historic villa, set in stunning gardens, offers breathtaking views of the coast and the sea. The rooms and suites are lavishly decorated, each with its own unique charm and character. Guests can dine at the hotel's gourmet restaurant, relax by the pool, or explore the beautiful gardens. The Villa Cimbrone also offers a range of activities, including cooking classes, wine tastings, and guided tours of the local area.

The Amalfi Coast offers a wide range of luxury hotels and resorts, each offering its own unique blend of comfort, elegance, and breathtaking views. Whether you are looking for a historic palace, a modern boutique hotel, or a serene retreat in a botanical garden, you are sure to find the perfect accommodation to make your visit to the Amalfi Coast an unforgettable experience.

Budget-Friendly Stays: Hostels and Guesthouses

Visiting the Amalfi Coast is a dream for many travelers, but it doesn't have to be an expensive one. There are plenty of budget-friendly accommodations, including hostels and guesthouses, that offer a comfortable and enjoyable stay without breaking the bank. These options allow you to experience the beauty and charm of the Amalfi Coast while keeping your travel expenses under control.

Hostels are a great choice for budget travelers, offering affordable rates and the chance to meet fellow travelers. One of the popular hostels in the area is A Scalinatella Hostel in Atrani. This cozy hostel is located in one of the smallest and most picturesque towns on the Amalfi Coast, just a short walk from Amalfi. The hostel offers both private rooms and dormitory beds, making it a flexible option for different budgets. Guests can enjoy the common areas, including a terrace with beautiful views, and the friendly atmosphere created by the helpful staff. Staying at A Scalinatella Hostel allows you to explore Atrani and its surroundings while enjoying a homely and welcoming environment.

Another excellent option is the Seven Hostel in Sant'Agnello, near Sorrento. While not directly on the Amalfi Coast, it is a convenient base for exploring the region. This stylish and modern hostel offers dormitory beds and private rooms at very reasonable prices. The rooftop terrace provides stunning views of the Bay of Naples and Mount Vesuvius, making it a great place to relax after a day of sightseeing. The hostel also has a bar and a restaurant, offering affordable meals and drinks. The Seven Hostel's location near the train station and bus stops makes it easy to travel to Sorrento, Positano, and other towns along the coast.

For those who prefer a more traditional Italian experience, guesthouses are a fantastic option. Guesthouses, or "affittacamere," are often family-run and provide a more personal touch. One such place is Casa Teresa in Positano. This charming guesthouse offers a range of rooms, each uniquely decorated in a traditional style. Guests can enjoy stunning views of the sea and the town from the balconies and terraces. The warm hospitality of the owners and the homemade breakfast featuring local ingredients add to the authentic experience. Staying at Casa Teresa allows you to immerse yourself in the local culture while enjoying the comforts of home.

In Amalfi, the Villa Maria Guesthouse is a great budget-friendly choice. Located in the heart of the town, this guesthouse provides easy access to the main attractions, including the Amalfi Cathedral and the beautiful beaches. The rooms are simple but comfortable, each with its own private bathroom. The guesthouse also offers a shared kitchen where guests can prepare their own meals, helping to save on dining expenses. The friendly and helpful hosts are always ready to provide tips and recommendations for exploring the area.

Ravello, known for its stunning views and beautiful gardens, also has budget-friendly options like Il Ducato di Ravello. This guesthouse is located close to the main square and offers comfortable rooms at reasonable rates. Guests can enjoy a complimentary breakfast on the terrace, overlooking the picturesque landscape. The guesthouse's central location makes it easy to explore Ravello's attractions, such as Villa Rufolo and Villa Cimbrone, without spending a lot on transportation.

For travelers who enjoy a more communal atmosphere, B&Bs (bed and breakfasts) are an excellent option. One notable B&B is Mamma Rosa in Positano. This family-run establishment offers comfortable rooms with stunning views of the sea and the town. The owners, Rosa and Carlo, provide a warm welcome and a delicious homemade breakfast each morning. The steep climb to reach Mamma Rosa is rewarded with incredible views and a peaceful setting away from the busy tourist areas. Staying here allows you to experience the hospitality and warmth of a traditional Italian family home.

In Praiano, a more laid-back town on the Amalfi Coast, the Locanda degli Dei is a charming B&B that offers great value for money. This cozy establishment has beautifully decorated rooms, each with its own private terrace or balcony. The friendly hosts serve a hearty breakfast each morning, which can be enjoyed while taking in the breathtaking views of the sea. The location of Locanda degli Dei provides easy access to hiking trails and the beautiful beaches of Praiano, making it an ideal base for nature lovers.

Another great budget option in Positano is the Hostel Brikette. This hostel offers dormitory beds and private rooms with stunning views of the coastline. The rooftop terrace is a highlight, providing a perfect spot to relax and socialize with other travelers. The hostel also has a bar and a communal kitchen, allowing guests to prepare their own meals and save on dining costs. The friendly staff at Hostel Brikette are always ready to provide tips and advice on exploring Positano and the surrounding areas.

For a unique and affordable stay, consider the Beata Solitudo in Agerola. This guesthouse is located in a former monastery and offers both dormitory beds and private rooms. The peaceful and serene setting provides a perfect escape from the busier towns along the coast. Agerola is known for its hiking trails, including the famous Path of the Gods, making it an excellent base for outdoor enthusiasts. The guesthouse also offers a communal kitchen and a lovely garden where guests can relax and enjoy the tranquil surroundings.

In Maiori, the Residence Due Torri offers affordable apartments with kitchen facilities, allowing guests to prepare their own meals and save on dining costs. The apartments are spacious and well-equipped, providing all the comforts of home. The location, just a short walk from the beach and the town center, makes it a convenient base for exploring Maiori and the nearby towns along the coast.

Amalfi Coast offers a variety of budget-friendly accommodations, including hostels, guesthouses, and B&Bs, that provide comfortable and enjoyable stays without breaking the bank. Whether you prefer the communal atmosphere of a hostel, the personal touch of a guesthouse, or the charm of a B&B, there are plenty of options to suit different preferences and budgets. By choosing budget-friendly accommodations, you can experience the beauty and charm of the Amalfi Coast while keeping your travel expenses under control, allowing you to make the most of your trip to this stunning region.

Family-Friendly Accommodations

Traveling with family to the Amalfi Coast is a delightful experience, offering stunning views, charming towns, and a rich cultural heritage. Finding the right accommodation that caters to the needs of families can significantly enhance the enjoyment of your trip. The Amalfi Coast boasts a variety of family-friendly accommodations, ranging from spacious hotels to cozy apartments, each providing a welcoming environment for travelers with children.

One of the top choices for family accommodations is the Hotel Margherita in Praiano. This hotel offers spacious family rooms and suites equipped with modern amenities. The hotel's location provides easy access to local attractions and beautiful beaches. It features a large swimming pool where children can have fun while parents relax on the sun terrace. The on-site restaurant serves delicious local cuisine, and the friendly staff are always ready to assist with special requests, such as providing cribs or arranging babysitting services. The hotel's complimentary shuttle service to the beach and nearby towns adds to its convenience for families. In Positano, the Villa Fiorentino is an excellent option for families looking for a more private and homely stay. This property offers a range of self-catering apartments and villas, each with a fully equipped kitchen, allowing families to prepare their own meals if they wish. The accommodations are spacious, featuring multiple bedrooms and living areas, making them perfect for families. The property's swimming pools, including one specifically for children, and the beautiful garden provide plenty of space for kids to play and parents to relax. The breathtaking views of Positano and the Mediterranean Sea from the terraces are an added bonus.

Amalfi is home to the family-friendly Hotel Aurora, which offers a variety of rooms and suites suitable for families. The hotel's location, right by the beach and close to the town center, makes it easy for families to explore the area. The hotel's private beach is equipped with sunbeds and umbrellas, providing a safe and comfortable environment for children to enjoy the sea. The hotel's restaurant offers a special children's menu, and the attentive staff are always on hand to make dining with kids a pleasant experience. The hotel also provides babysitting services upon request.

For families seeking a luxurious stay, the Belmond Hotel Caruso in Ravello is an ideal choice. This historic hotel, set in a restored 11th-century palace, offers family suites that are both spacious and elegantly decorated. The hotel's infinity pool, with its stunning views of the coastline, is a favorite among families. The hotel also offers a Kids' Club, where children can participate in various activities and games under the supervision of trained staff, allowing parents to enjoy some relaxing time on their own. The hotel's gardens and terraces provide plenty of space for children to explore and play.

In Minori, the Villa Romana Hotel & Spa is another great option for families. This hotel offers family rooms and interconnected suites, providing ample space for everyone. The hotel's location, close to the beach and the town's main attractions, makes it convenient for families to explore. The on-site restaurant offers a children's menu, and the hotel's large outdoor swimming pool is perfect for kids to enjoy. The spa facilities provide a chance for parents to unwind while the children are entertained with various activities.

The Hotel Buca di Bacco in Positano is renowned for its family-friendly atmosphere. This beachfront hotel offers rooms and suites that can accommodate families of different sizes. The hotel's location, right on the Spiaggia Grande beach, provides easy access to the sea and various water activities. The hotel's restaurant serves a wide range of dishes, including options for children. The friendly staff are always available to help with any special requests, such as arranging excursions or providing extra bedding for children.

In Maiori, the Residence Due Torri is a great choice for families looking for apartment-style accommodations. The property offers spacious apartments with fully equipped kitchens, allowing families to prepare their own meals if they prefer. The apartments are modern and comfortable, with plenty of space for children to play. The location, just a short walk from the beach and the town center, makes it easy for families to explore Maiori and its surroundings. The property also offers a rooftop terrace with stunning views, providing a perfect spot for families to relax and enjoy the scenery.

For a unique and memorable stay, families can consider the Agriturismo Mare e Monti in Furore. This family-run farmhouse offers a range of accommodations, from rooms to apartments, all with beautiful views of the sea and the surrounding countryside. The property features a large garden with a playground, making it an ideal place for children to play. The on-site restaurant serves homemade dishes prepared with ingredients from the farm, providing a true taste of local cuisine. The friendly hosts are always ready to offer tips and advice on exploring the area, ensuring a pleasant stay for the entire family.

The Amalfi Coast offers a wide range of family-friendly accommodations that cater to the needs of travelers with children. Whether you prefer the convenience of a hotel, the privacy of an apartment, or the charm of a farmhouse, there are plenty of options to choose from. By selecting the right accommodation, you can ensure a comfortable and enjoyable stay for the entire family, allowing you to make the most of your visit to this beautiful region. From spacious rooms and kid-friendly amenities to convenient locations and welcoming hosts, these family-friendly accommodations provide the perfect base for exploring the Amalfi Coast and creating lasting memories with your loved ones.

Romantic Getaways: Boutique Hotels and Villas

The Amalfi Coast is an ideal destination for romantic getaways, offering breathtaking landscapes, charming towns, and a rich cultural heritage. For couples seeking an intimate and luxurious experience, boutique hotels and private villas provide the perfect setting. These accommodations combine comfort, elegance, and personalized service to create unforgettable memories.

Boutique hotels on the Amalfi Coast offer a unique blend of charm and luxury. One of the most renowned options is Le Sirenuse in Positano. This iconic hotel, once a private residence, is now a symbol of refined elegance. The rooms and suites are individually decorated with antique furnishings and vibrant colors, creating a romantic and cozy atmosphere. Each room offers stunning views of the Mediterranean Sea and the picturesque town of Positano. Couples can enjoy a romantic dinner at the Michelin-starred restaurant La Sponda, where the candlelit ambiance and exquisite cuisine set the stage for a memorable evening. The hotel's amenities, including a beautiful swimming pool, a spa, and a private boat for excursions, ensure a luxurious and relaxing stay.

Another top choice is the Belmond Hotel Caruso in Ravello. Perched high on a cliff, this historic hotel offers breathtaking views of the coastline. The rooms and suites are elegantly decorated with antique furniture and modern comforts, providing a serene and romantic setting. The hotel's infinity pool, overlooking the sea, is one of the most iconic spots on the Amalfi Coast. Couples can enjoy a romantic dinner at the hotel's restaurant, which serves delicious Mediterranean cuisine. The hotel's lush gardens, spa, and personalized service make it an ideal choice for a romantic getaway.

In Amalfi, the Santa Caterina Hotel is a beautiful boutique hotel that combines classic elegance with modern luxury. The rooms and suites are decorated in a traditional style, with hand-painted tiles and antique furnishings. Each room offers stunning views of the sea and the surrounding landscape. The hotel's private beach club, accessible by elevator, provides a secluded spot for couples to relax and enjoy the sun. The hotel's restaurant, Glicine, offers a romantic dining experience with panoramic views of the coast. The Santa Caterina Hotel also features a spa, a swimming pool, and beautiful gardens, making it a perfect choice for a romantic escape.

For those seeking a more private and exclusive experience, villas on the Amalfi Coast offer the ultimate in luxury and romance. Villa Treville in Positano is a stunning private estate that offers a unique and personalized experience. The villa's suites are individually decorated, each with its own unique style and character. The estate features beautiful gardens, terraces, and a private beach, providing plenty of space for couples to relax and enjoy the breathtaking views. The villa's staff provides exceptional service, including personalized dining experiences and private boat excursions, ensuring a truly unforgettable stay.

Another excellent option is Villa Cimbrone in Ravello. This historic villa, set in stunning gardens, offers a unique blend of history and luxury. The rooms and suites are beautifully decorated, with antique furnishings and modern amenities. The villa's gardens, which are open to the public during the day, provide a romantic setting for a stroll or a private picnic. The villa's restaurant, Il Flauto di Pan, offers a gourmet dining experience with stunning views of the coastline. The Villa Cimbrone also features a swimming pool and a spa, making it a perfect choice for a romantic getaway.

In Praiano, Casa Angelina is a modern boutique hotel that offers a sleek and contemporary setting for a romantic retreat. The rooms and suites are bright and airy, with minimalist decor and stunning views of the sea. The hotel's rooftop terrace is a highlight, offering panoramic views of the coast and a perfect spot for enjoying a cocktail at sunset. The hotel's restaurant, Un Piano nel Cielo, offers gourmet Mediterranean cuisine in a romantic setting. The Casa Angelina also features a spa, a swimming pool, and direct access to a private beach, making it an ideal choice for couples seeking a luxurious and intimate escape.

For a more traditional and rustic experience, the Torre di Cesare in Maiori is a charming boutique hotel set in a restored medieval tower. The rooms are individually decorated, with antique furnishings and modern amenities. The hotel's terraces offer stunning views of the sea and the surrounding landscape, providing a romantic setting for a private dinner or a relaxing evening. The Torre di Cesare also features a swimming pool and beautiful gardens, making it a perfect choice for a romantic getaway.

The Amalfi Coast offers a wide range of romantic boutique hotels and villas that provide the perfect setting for a memorable getaway. Whether you prefer the elegance of a historic hotel, the modern luxury of a boutique hotel, or the privacy of a private villa, there are plenty of options to choose from. By selecting the right accommodation, you can ensure a comfortable and enjoyable stay, allowing you to create lasting memories with your loved one. From stunning views and luxurious amenities to personalized service and romantic dining experiences, these boutique hotels and villas offer everything you need for the perfect romantic retreat on the Amalfi Coast.

Unique Stays: B&Bs and Farmhouses

The Amalfi Coast is renowned for its stunning scenery, charming towns, and rich cultural heritage. While luxury hotels and resorts are popular choices for many tourists, those seeking a more authentic and unique experience often opt for bed and breakfasts (B&Bs) and farmhouses. These accommodations offer a more intimate and personalized stay, often with the added benefit of being immersed in the local culture and lifestyle.

B&Bs and farmhouses, often family-run, provide a warm and welcoming environment that larger hotels cannot match. One of the most charming B&Bs on the Amalfi Coast is Villa Maria Antonietta in Positano. This delightful B&B offers stunning views of the sea and the colorful town of Positano. The rooms are tastefully decorated, each with its own unique character, providing a cozy and comfortable atmosphere. The hosts are known for their hospitality, serving a delicious homemade breakfast each morning on the terrace, where guests can enjoy the breathtaking views. Staying at Villa Maria Antonietta allows you to experience the charm and beauty of Positano in a relaxed and friendly setting.

Another excellent choice is the B&B Casa Nilde in Positano. This family-run B&B offers spacious rooms with balconies overlooking the sea. The modern and elegant decor creates a comfortable and inviting atmosphere. The hosts go out of their way to make guests feel at home, providing helpful tips and recommendations for exploring the area. The highlight of a stay at Casa Nilde is the breakfast, featuring fresh local produce and served on a terrace with panoramic views of the coastline. The central location makes it easy to explore Positano and its many attractions.

In Ravello, the Palazzo della Marra is a historic B&B that offers a unique and memorable stay. Housed in a restored medieval building, this B&B combines historical charm with modern comforts. The rooms are beautifully decorated, with antique furnishings and original architectural details. The rooftop terrace offers stunning views of the coast and is the perfect spot to relax and take in the scenery. The hosts are known for their warm hospitality, providing a delicious breakfast each morning and offering valuable insights into the local area. Staying at Palazzo della Marra allows you to step back in time and experience the rich history of Ravello.

For those seeking a more rural and tranquil experience, farmhouses on the Amalfi Coast offer a unique and authentic stay. Agriturismo Sant'Alfonso in Furore is a wonderful example. This farmhouse is set in the hills above the coast, surrounded by vineyards and olive groves. The rooms are rustic yet comfortable, offering stunning views of the sea and the countryside. Guests can enjoy homemade meals prepared with ingredients grown on the farm, providing a true taste of local cuisine. The peaceful and serene setting makes it an ideal place to relax and unwind, away from the hustle and bustle of the coastal towns.

Another excellent farmhouse is Agriturismo Mare e Monti in Agerola. This family-run establishment offers a range of accommodations, from rooms to apartments, all with beautiful views of the sea and the surrounding countryside. The property features a large garden with a playground, making it an ideal place for families. The on-site restaurant serves homemade dishes prepared with ingredients from the farm, providing a true taste of local cuisine. The friendly hosts are always ready to offer tips and advice on exploring the area, ensuring a pleasant stay for the entire family.

For a truly unique experience, consider staying at Agriturismo La Selva in Positano. This farmhouse is perched high above the town, offering breathtaking views of the sea and the Amalfi Coast. The accommodations are simple but comfortable, with private terraces overlooking the stunning scenery. Guests can participate in activities such as cooking classes, wine tastings, and guided hikes, providing an immersive experience of the local culture and lifestyle. The on-site restaurant serves delicious meals made with fresh, organic ingredients grown on the farm, ensuring a memorable dining experience.

In Minori, the Torre dello Ziro is a charming B&B set in a historic tower. This unique accommodation offers a blend of history and modern comforts, with beautifully decorated rooms and stunning views of the sea. The hosts provide a warm and welcoming atmosphere, serving a delicious breakfast each morning and offering helpful tips for exploring the area. The central location makes it easy to explore Minori and the nearby towns along the coast.

For a more intimate and personalized stay, consider the Casa Teresa in Positano. This charming guesthouse offers a range of rooms, each uniquely decorated in a traditional style.

Guests can enjoy stunning views of the sea and the town from the balconies and terraces. The warm hospitality of the owners and the homemade breakfast featuring local ingredients add to the authentic experience. Staying at Casa Teresa allows you to immerse yourself in the local culture while enjoying the comforts of home.

Another excellent option is the B&B Mamma Rosa in Positano. This family-run establishment offers comfortable rooms with stunning views of the sea and the town. The owners, Rosa and Carlo, provide a warm welcome and a delicious homemade breakfast each morning. The steep climb to reach Mamma Rosa is rewarded with incredible views and a peaceful setting away from the busy tourist areas. Staying here allows you to experience the hospitality and warmth of a traditional Italian family home.

In Praiano, the Locanda degli Dei is a charming B&B that offers great value for money. This cozy establishment has beautifully decorated rooms, each with its own private terrace or balcony. The friendly hosts serve a hearty breakfast each morning, which can be enjoyed while taking in the breathtaking views of the sea. The location of Locanda degli Dei provides easy access to hiking trails and the beautiful beaches of Praiano, making it an ideal base for nature lovers.

Finally, in Maiori, the Residence Due Torri offers affordable apartments with kitchen facilities, allowing guests to prepare their own meals and save on dining costs. The apartments are spacious and well-equipped, providing all the comforts of home. The location, just a short walk from the beach and the town center, makes it a convenient base for exploring Maiori and its surroundings. The property also offers a rooftop terrace with stunning views, providing a perfect spot for families to relax and enjoy the scenery.

Amalfi Coast offers a wide range of unique and memorable B&Bs and farmhouses that provide a more intimate and personalized stay. Whether you prefer the charm of a historic B&B, the tranquility of a farmhouse, or the warmth of a family-run guesthouse, there are plenty of options to suit different preferences and budgets. By choosing these unique accommodations, you can experience the beauty and charm of the Amalfi Coast while enjoying the comforts of home and the hospitality of local hosts. This ensures a truly special and unforgettable visit to this stunning region.

CHAPTER 5

TOP ATTRACTIONS AND SIGHTSEEING

Must-See Landmarks

Amalfi Cathedral

The Amalfi Cathedral, also known as the Cathedral of St. Andrew or Duomo di Amalfi, is one of the most iconic and must-see landmarks on the Amalfi Coast. Located in the heart of the town of Amalfi, this stunning cathedral is not only a place of worship but also a historical and architectural marvel that attracts countless visitors each year. Its rich history, striking architecture, and cultural significance make it a top attraction for tourists exploring the region.

The Amalfi Cathedral's history dates back to the 9th century when it was first constructed. Over the centuries, the cathedral has undergone numerous renovations and expansions, resulting in the unique blend of architectural styles seen today. The most prominent of these styles are Romanesque, Baroque, and Byzantine, each contributing to the cathedral's distinctive appearance. The cathedral is dedicated to Saint Andrew, the patron saint of Amalfi, whose relics are housed within the church.

As you approach the Amalfi Cathedral, the first thing that catches your eye is the grand staircase leading up to the main entrance. This imposing staircase, consisting of 62 steps, adds to the cathedral's majestic presence and offers a striking view of the town's main square, Piazza del Duomo. The staircase is often bustling with tourists and locals, providing a lively atmosphere that contrasts with the serene interior of the cathedral.

The façade of the Amalfi Cathedral is a masterpiece in itself. The current façade, rebuilt in the 19th century after the original was damaged in an earthquake, is an excellent example of the neo-Moorish style. It features intricate mosaics, pointed arches, and detailed carvings that captivate visitors. The mosaic in the central tympanum, depicting Christ enthroned with saints and angels, is particularly impressive and adds to the grandeur of the entrance.

Stepping inside the Amalfi Cathedral, visitors are greeted by the breathtaking interior that reflects the church's long and diverse history. The nave is flanked by two aisles separated by rows of columns, and the ceiling is adorned with beautiful frescoes depicting scenes from the life of Saint Andrew. The Baroque influence is evident in the elaborate decoration, including gilded stucco work and intricate wood carvings. The central nave leads to the high altar, which is a focal point of the cathedral's interior. The altar is made of marble and is intricately decorated with precious stones and metals, creating a stunning centerpiece.

One of the most significant features of the Amalfi Cathedral is the crypt of Saint Andrew. The crypt, located beneath the main altar, is the final resting place of the apostle's relics, which were brought to Amalfi in the 13th century from Constantinople. The crypt is a sacred space that draws pilgrims from around the world. It is richly decorated with frescoes and stucco work, and the air is filled with a sense of reverence and awe. Visitors can descend into the crypt to view the reliquary that holds the remains of Saint Andrew, making it a deeply spiritual experience.

Adjacent to the cathedral is the Cloister of Paradise (Chiostro del Paradiso), another must-see attraction. The cloister was built in the 13th century as a burial ground for Amalfi's noble families. Its design is influenced by Islamic architecture, featuring elegant arches and columns surrounding a peaceful garden. The cloister provides a tranquil escape from the bustling town and offers a glimpse into the historical and cultural fusion that characterizes Amalfi. The garden, with its lush greenery and ancient sarcophagi, is a perfect spot for reflection and relaxation.

The Amalfi Cathedral also houses a museum that showcases a collection of religious artifacts, artwork, and historical documents. The museum provides a deeper understanding of the cathedral's history and its significance to the town of Amalfi. Exhibits include ancient manuscripts, liturgical objects, and pieces of art that highlight the cathedral's role in the religious and cultural life of the region. The museum is an essential visit for those interested in the rich heritage of Amalfi and its cathedral.

Visiting the Amalfi Cathedral is not only about admiring its architectural beauty but also about understanding its cultural and historical importance. The cathedral has been a central part of Amalfi's identity for over a millennium, serving as a place of worship, a repository of relics, and a symbol of the town's resilience and faith. Its influence extends beyond the religious sphere, as it has played a vital role in the social and cultural development of Amalfi.

For tourists, the Amalfi Cathedral offers a comprehensive experience that combines history, art, and spirituality. It stands as a testament to the town's rich past and its enduring significance. Whether you are an art enthusiast, a history buff, or a spiritual seeker, the cathedral provides a wealth of knowledge and inspiration. Its majestic presence, intricate details, and profound significance make it a highlight of any visit to the Amalfi Coast.

The Amalfi Cathedral is a must-see landmark and top attraction for tourists on the Amalfi Coast. Its rich history, stunning architecture, and cultural significance make it an essential stop for anyone exploring the region. From the grand staircase and striking façade to the breathtaking interior and sacred crypt, the cathedral offers a deeply enriching experience. Visitors are invited to immerse themselves in the beauty, history, and spirituality of this iconic landmark, ensuring that their visit to the Amalfi Coast is truly memorable.

Villa Rufolo

Villa Rufolo, located in the charming town of Ravello on the Amalfi Coast, is one of the most remarkable landmarks in the region. Known for its stunning architecture, beautiful gardens, and breathtaking views, Villa Rufolo is a must-see attraction for tourists. Its rich history and cultural significance make it a highlight of any visit to the Amalfi Coast.

The history of Villa Rufolo dates back to the 13th century when it was built by the wealthy Rufolo family, who were prominent merchants in the region. The villa was designed to showcase the family's wealth and power, and it quickly became a center of social and cultural life in Ravello. Over the centuries, the villa has seen many changes and renovations, but it has always retained its unique charm and beauty.

As you approach Villa Rufolo, you are immediately struck by its impressive entrance. The main gate, adorned with intricate carvings and surrounded by lush greenery, sets the tone for what lies within. The villa's architecture is a blend of Arab, Norman, and Gothic styles, reflecting the diverse influences that have shaped the region over the centuries. This fusion of styles is evident in the arches, columns, and decorative elements that adorn the villa's facade.

Upon entering the villa, visitors are greeted by a picturesque courtyard, which is the heart of the complex. The courtyard is surrounded by a series of arcades and loggias, each beautifully decorated with mosaics and frescoes. The central fountain, with its elegant design and soothing water features, adds to the serene atmosphere of the space. The courtyard is a perfect spot to sit and relax, taking in the beauty and tranquility of the surroundings.

One of the main attractions of Villa Rufolo is its gardens, which are among the most beautiful on the Amalfi Coast. The gardens were originally designed in the 19th century by the Scottish botanist Sir Francis Neville Reid, who transformed the villa's grounds into a botanical masterpiece. The gardens are divided into several terraces, each offering stunning views of the coastline and the sea. The lower terrace is known for its lush greenery and vibrant flowers, while the upper terrace provides panoramic views that are truly breathtaking.

The gardens are meticulously maintained and feature a wide variety of plants and flowers, including roses, bougainvillea, and Mediterranean herbs. Walking through the gardens, visitors can enjoy the fragrant scents and vibrant colors that change with the seasons. The pathways wind through the gardens, leading to hidden corners and secluded spots where you can sit and enjoy the peaceful surroundings.

One of the most iconic features of Villa Rufolo is the Belvedere, a terrace that offers spectacular views of the Amalfi Coast. The Belvedere is framed by two tall towers, which were once part of the villa's defensive structure. From this vantage point, you can see the dramatic cliffs, the sparkling sea, and the charming towns that dot the coastline. The view from the Belvedere is one of the most photographed spots on the Amalfi Coast, and it is easy to see why. The combination of natural beauty and architectural elegance creates a scene that is both awe-inspiring and serene.

Villa Rufolo is also known for its cultural events and festivals, which attract visitors from around the world. The most famous of these is the Ravello Festival, an annual music and arts festival that takes place in the villa's gardens and other locations in Ravello. The festival was founded in 1953 in honor of the composer Richard Wagner, who was inspired by the beauty of Villa Rufolo during his visit in 1880. The festival features a wide range of performances, including classical music, opera, ballet, and jazz, as well as art exhibitions and literary events. The combination of world-class performances and the stunning setting of Villa Rufolo makes the Ravello Festival a truly unique and unforgettable experience.

In addition to its gardens and cultural events, Villa Rufolo also houses a museum that showcases the villa's history and the art and artifacts associated with it. The museum features a collection of medieval and Renaissance art, including paintings, sculptures, and ceramics. The exhibits provide a fascinating insight into the history of Ravello and the cultural heritage of the Amalfi Coast. The museum is a must-visit for anyone interested in art and history, offering a deeper understanding of the significance of Villa Rufolo and its place in the region's history.

Visiting Villa Rufolo is not just about admiring its beauty and history; it is also about experiencing the sense of peace and tranquility that pervades the place. The villa and its gardens offer a respite from the hustle and bustle of everyday life, providing a space where you can relax and reconnect with nature. Whether you are strolling through the gardens, sitting in the courtyard, or gazing out at the sea from the Belvedere, Villa Rufolo offers a sense of serenity and timelessness that is truly special.

Villa Rufolo is a must-see landmark and top attraction for tourists on the Amalfi Coast. Its rich history, stunning architecture, and beautiful gardens make it a highlight of any visit to the region. The villa's blend of Arab, Norman, and Gothic styles, combined with its lush gardens and breathtaking views, create a unique and enchanting atmosphere. Whether you are interested in history, art, music, or simply enjoying the beauty of nature, Villa Rufolo offers something for everyone. Its cultural significance and serene setting make it a place that leaves a lasting impression on all who visit, ensuring that your time on the Amalfi Coast is truly unforgettable.

Villa Cimbrone

Villa Cimbrone, located in the charming town of Ravello on the Amalfi Coast, is a breathtaking landmark and a top attraction for tourists visiting the region. Renowned for its stunning gardens, impressive architecture, and panoramic views, Villa Cimbrone offers a unique and unforgettable experience. Its rich history, combined with its beauty, makes it an essential destination for anyone exploring the Amalfi Coast.

The history of Villa Cimbrone dates back to at least the 11th century when it was part of a vast estate owned by the aristocratic Acconciajoco family. Over the centuries, the villa has undergone numerous changes and renovations, particularly in the early 20th century when it was transformed by the English nobleman Ernest William Beckett, Lord Grimthorpe. Beckett, inspired by his travels and love of art and architecture, sought to create a place that combined elements of different cultures and styles. He employed the help of local artisans and craftsmen to bring his vision to life, resulting in the eclectic and enchanting Villa Cimbrone we see today.

As you approach Villa Cimbrone, the first thing you notice is the imposing entrance gate, adorned with intricate carvings and surrounded by lush greenery. This grand entrance sets the tone for the experience that awaits inside. The path leading to the villa is lined with beautiful flowers and trees, creating a sense of anticipation and wonder. The villa itself is a masterpiece of architectural styles, blending elements of Gothic, Moorish, and Renaissance design. This fusion of styles is evident in the arches, columns, and decorative details that adorn the building.

One of the main attractions of Villa Cimbrone is its spectacular gardens, which are among the most beautiful on the Amalfi Coast. The gardens, originally designed by Lord Grimthorpe, are meticulously maintained and feature a wide variety of plants and flowers, including roses, wisteria, and Mediterranean herbs. The gardens are divided into several sections, each with its own unique charm and character. Walking through the gardens, visitors can enjoy the fragrant scents and vibrant colors that change with the seasons. The pathways wind through the gardens, leading to hidden corners and secluded spots where you can sit and enjoy the peaceful surroundings.

The centerpiece of Villa Cimbrone is the Terrazza dell'Infinito, or Terrace of Infinity. This terrace offers one of the most breathtaking views on the Amalfi Coast, with its marble busts and panoramic vistas of the coastline and the Mediterranean Sea. The view from the Terrace of Infinity is truly awe-inspiring, providing a sense of boundless beauty and tranquility. It is no wonder that this spot has been a favorite of artists, writers, and travelers for centuries. The terrace is particularly stunning at sunrise and sunset when the light casts a magical glow over the landscape.

Villa Cimbrone is also home to several other notable features, including the Crypt, the Temple of Ceres, and the Avenue of Immensity. The Crypt, located beneath the villa, is a Gothic-style structure that serves as a peaceful and reflective space. Its arched ceilings and stone columns create a sense of grandeur and solemnity. The Temple of Ceres, dedicated to the Roman goddess of agriculture, is a charming structure that adds to the villa's classical ambiance. The Avenue of Immensity is a long, tree-lined pathway that offers stunning views of the gardens and the sea, providing a perfect spot for a leisurely stroll.

The cultural significance of Villa Cimbrone is further enhanced by its connection to various historical figures and events. The villa has hosted many notable guests over the years, including Virginia Woolf, Winston Churchill, and Greta Garbo, who were drawn to its beauty and serenity. The villa has also been a source of inspiration for numerous artists and writers, who have captured its essence in their works. The rich history and cultural heritage of Villa Cimbrone make it a place of great significance and allure.

In addition to its historical and cultural significance, Villa Cimbrone is also a popular venue for events and celebrations. The villa's stunning gardens and elegant interiors provide a perfect setting for weddings, receptions, and other special occasions. The combination of natural beauty and architectural splendor creates an unforgettable backdrop for any event. The villa's staff are known for their attention to detail and exceptional service, ensuring that every event is a memorable and magical experience.

Visiting Villa Cimbrone is not just about admiring its beauty and history; it is also about experiencing the sense of peace and tranquility that pervades the place. The villa and its gardens offer a respite from the hustle and bustle of everyday life, providing a space where you can relax and reconnect with nature. Whether you are strolling through the gardens, sitting on the Terrace of Infinity, or exploring the villa's many features, Villa Cimbrone offers a sense of serenity and timelessness that is truly special.

For tourists, Villa Cimbrone offers a comprehensive experience that combines history, art, and nature. It stands as a testament to the creativity and vision of those who have shaped it over the centuries. Whether you are an art enthusiast, a history buff, or simply someone who appreciates natural beauty, Villa Cimbrone provides a wealth of knowledge and inspiration. Its majestic presence, intricate details, and profound significance make it a highlight of any visit to the Amalfi Coast.

Villa Cimbrone is a must-see landmark and top attraction for tourists on the Amalfi Coast. Its rich history, stunning architecture, and beautiful gardens make it an essential stop for anyone exploring the region. From the imposing entrance gate and grand pathways to the breathtaking Terrace of Infinity and the serene gardens, Villa Cimbrone offers a deeply enriching experience. Visitors are invited to immerse themselves in the beauty, history, and tranquility of this iconic landmark, ensuring that their visit to the Amalfi Coast is truly unforgettable.

Hidden Gems and Off-the-Beaten-Path Spots

The Amalfi Coast is famous for its breathtaking scenery, charming towns, and rich cultural heritage. While popular spots like Positano, Amalfi, and Ravello draw countless tourists, there are numerous hidden gems and off-the-beaten-path locations that offer a more intimate and unique experience. These lesser-known spots provide an opportunity to escape the crowds and explore the true essence of the Amalfi Coast.

One of the most enchanting hidden gems on the Amalfi Coast is the town of Atrani. Nestled between the cliffs and the sea, Atrani is one of the smallest and most picturesque towns in Italy. Its narrow streets, charming squares, and historic buildings create a timeless atmosphere. The town's main square, Piazza Umberto I, is a lively hub where locals gather to socialize and relax. The Church of San Salvatore de' Birecto, with its beautiful Byzantine façade, is a must-visit. Atrani's beach, less crowded than those in nearby towns, offers a peaceful spot to enjoy the sun and sea.

Another lesser-known treasure is the village of Furore, famous for its stunning fjord, Fiordo di Furore. This natural wonder, with its dramatic cliffs and turquoise waters, is a hidden paradise. The fjord is home to a small beach and a picturesque fishing village, providing a serene escape from the more touristy areas. A walk along the path that leads to the fjord offers breathtaking views of the coastline and the sea. Furore is also known for its vibrant murals that adorn the village walls, adding a unique artistic touch to the area.

In the hills above the Amalfi Coast lies the charming town of Scala. Known as the oldest town on the coast, Scala offers a glimpse into the region's rich history. The town's medieval architecture, narrow alleys, and historic churches create a captivating atmosphere. The Cathedral of San Lorenzo, with its impressive Romanesque façade and beautiful interior, is a highlight. Scala is also a gateway to some of the best hiking trails in the region, including the trail to the Valle delle Ferriere, a lush nature reserve with waterfalls and rare plant species.

For those seeking a more tranquil beach experience, the Spiaggia di Erchie is a hidden gem worth exploring. This secluded beach, located between Amalfi and Salerno, is surrounded by cliffs and lush vegetation, creating a peaceful and picturesque setting. The clear, calm waters are perfect for swimming and snorkeling. The village of Erchie, with its charming houses and narrow streets, adds to the beach's appeal. The beach is relatively uncrowded, even during peak season, making it an ideal spot for a relaxing day by the sea.

Another off-the-beaten-path spot is the village of Conca dei Marini, known for its stunning coastal views and traditional charm. The village is famous for the Grotta dello Smeraldo, or Emerald Grotto, a sea cave filled with mesmerizing green light. A visit to the grotto, accessible by boat or stairs, is a magical experience. Conca dei Marini is also home to the Torre del Capo di Conca, a historic watchtower offering panoramic views of the coastline. The village's narrow streets, lined with whitewashed houses and vibrant flowers, provide a picturesque setting for a leisurely stroll.

In the hills above Praiano, the Path of the Gods (Sentiero degli Dei) is one of the most spectacular hiking trails on the Amalfi Coast. This trail offers breathtaking views of the coastline, the sea, and the surrounding mountains. The trail begins in the village of Bomerano and ends in Nocelle, a hamlet above Positano. Along the way, hikers pass through terraced vineyards, ancient ruins, and charming villages. The trail is well-marked and accessible to hikers of all levels, making it a must-do for nature lovers and adventure seekers.

For a unique cultural experience, the town of Minori offers a glimpse into the culinary traditions of the Amalfi Coast. Minori is known as the "City of Taste" and is famous for its delicious pastries and pasta. A visit to a local pasticceria, such as Sal De Riso, provides an opportunity to sample traditional sweets like delizia al limone and sfogliatella. Minori is also home to the ancient Roman Villa Marittima, an archaeological site with well-preserved mosaics and frescoes. The town's annual GustaMinori festival celebrates local food, wine, and culture, providing a lively and authentic experience.

In the heart of the Amalfi Coast, the village of Tramonti is a hidden gem known for its scenic beauty and rich agricultural heritage. Tramonti is surrounded by terraced vineyards and lemon groves, offering a picturesque setting for a leisurely visit. The village is famous for its traditional pizza, made with locally grown ingredients and cooked in wood-fired ovens. A visit to one of Tramonti's pizzerias, such as Pizzeria San Francisco, is a must for food lovers. The village is also home to several historic churches and monasteries, including the Church of San Pietro Apostolo and the Convent of San Francesco.

For those interested in history and architecture, the town of Vietri sul Mare is a hidden treasure on the Amalfi Coast. Vietri sul Mare is renowned for its vibrant ceramics, which have been produced in the town for centuries. The town's colorful ceramics adorn the buildings, streets, and shops, creating a lively and artistic atmosphere. A visit to the Ceramics Museum, housed in the historic Villa Guariglia, provides insight into the town's rich ceramic tradition. The town's main church, the Church of San Giovanni Battista, features a stunning majolica-tiled dome and beautiful interior decorations.

In the hills above Amalfi, the village of Pogerola offers a peaceful retreat with stunning views of the coastline. Pogerola is known for its charming streets, historic buildings, and friendly locals. The village's main square, Piazza Umberto I, is a lively hub where residents gather to socialize and enjoy the scenic views. The Church of San Michele Arcangelo, with its beautiful frescoes and serene atmosphere, is a must-visit. Pogerola is also a starting point for several hiking trails that lead to panoramic viewpoints and hidden spots in the surrounding hills.

The Amalfi Coast is home to numerous hidden gems and off-the-beaten-path spots that offer a unique and authentic experience. From charming villages and secluded beaches to scenic hiking trails and historic sites, these lesser-known destinations provide an opportunity to explore the true essence of the Amalfi Coast. Whether you are seeking tranquility, adventure, or cultural immersion, these hidden treasures offer a rich and rewarding experience that will enhance your visit to this stunning region.

Historical Sites and Museums

The Amalfi Coast is renowned for its stunning landscapes, charming villages, and rich cultural heritage. Among its many attractions, the historical sites and museums stand out as key highlights, offering visitors a deep dive into the region's fascinating past. These sites and museums provide invaluable insights into the history, art, and culture that have shaped the Amalfi Coast over centuries.

One of the most prominent historical sites on the Amalfi Coast is the Amalfi Cathedral, also known as the Cathedral of St. Andrew. Located in the heart of Amalfi, this stunning cathedral is a masterpiece of medieval architecture. It was originally built in the 9th century and has been expanded and renovated over the centuries, resulting in a blend of Romanesque, Baroque, and Byzantine styles. The cathedral is dedicated to Saint Andrew, whose relics are housed in the crypt beneath the main altar. Visitors can admire the beautiful façade, which features intricate mosaics and detailed carvings, before stepping inside to explore the richly decorated interior, complete with frescoes, gilded stucco work, and a stunning high altar.

Adjacent to the cathedral is the Cloister of Paradise, an elegant 13th-century cloister that served as a burial ground for Amalfi's noble families. The cloister is characterized by its Arab-Norman architecture, featuring slender columns and pointed arches that create a serene and contemplative atmosphere. The cloister's garden, with its palm trees and lush greenery, offers a peaceful escape from the bustling town. The adjoining cathedral museum displays a collection of religious artifacts, including ancient manuscripts, liturgical objects, and artworks that highlight the cathedral's historical and cultural significance.

In the town of Ravello, the Villa Rufolo is a must-visit historical site. This villa dates back to the 13th century and was originally built by the wealthy Rufolo family. The villa is renowned for its stunning gardens, which were designed in the 19th century by Sir Francis Neville Reid. The gardens are terraced, offering breathtaking views of the coastline and the Mediterranean Sea. Visitors can wander through the lush gardens, adorned with vibrant flowers, fountains, and statues, while enjoying the peaceful ambiance. The villa itself features a blend of architectural styles, including Gothic, Moorish, and Norman influences, and hosts cultural events and concerts throughout the year, most notably the Ravello Festival.

Another significant site in Ravello is the Villa Cimbrone, a historic villa with origins in the 11th century. The villa is famous for its stunning gardens and panoramic views from the Terrace of Infinity. The gardens, filled with statues, temples, and classical sculptures, reflect a blend of Italian and English landscaping traditions. The villa's interior features a mix of architectural styles, showcasing the artistic vision of its various owners. Villa Cimbrone's gardens are open to the public, offering a tranquil retreat and a chance to explore one of the Amalfi Coast's most beautiful settings.

In the town of Minori, the Roman Villa Marittima is an archaeological gem that offers a glimpse into the ancient history of the region. This well-preserved Roman villa dates back to the 1st century AD and was likely a luxurious seaside retreat for a wealthy Roman family. The villa features intricate mosaics, frescoes, and marble decorations that highlight the opulence of Roman life. Visitors can explore the remains of the villa, including its bath complex, living quarters, and beautiful gardens, while learning about the daily life and leisure activities of ancient Romans.

The town of Atrani is home to the Church of San Salvatore de' Birecto, a historical site with significant cultural importance. This church, originally built in the 10th century, features a beautiful Byzantine-style façade and an interior adorned with frescoes and mosaics. The church served as the coronation site for the Dukes of Amalfi, adding to its historical significance. Visitors can admire the church's architectural beauty and learn about its role in the region's history.

The Museum of Paper, located in Amalfi, offers a unique insight into the region's industrial heritage. Housed in a former paper mill, the museum showcases the history and techniques of traditional paper-making, an important industry in Amalfi since the 12th century. Visitors can see the original machinery and tools used in the production of handmade paper, as well as learn about the various stages of the paper-making process. The museum also features exhibits on the history of writing and printing, making it an informative and engaging experience for all ages.

For those interested in maritime history, the Amalfi Coast's Maritime Republic Museum in Amalfi is a must-visit. This museum is dedicated to the history of Amalfi as a powerful maritime republic during the Middle Ages. The exhibits include models of ancient ships, navigational instruments, and artifacts related to maritime trade and exploration. Visitors can learn about Amalfi's role in the development of maritime law, as well as its contributions to navigation and shipbuilding. The museum provides a comprehensive overview of the region's maritime heritage and its influence on the Mediterranean world.

In Positano, the Church of Santa Maria Assunta is a historical site that attracts many visitors. The church, with its iconic dome covered in majolica tiles, dates back to the 10th century. The interior of the church is richly decorated with marble and frescoes, and it houses the famous Byzantine icon of the Black Madonna. According to local legend, the icon was brought to Positano by pirates and has been a symbol of the town ever since. The church's beautiful architecture and intriguing history make it a significant cultural landmark on the Amalfi Coast.

The town of Vietri sul Mare is famous for its ceramics, and the Ceramics Museum housed in Villa Guariglia is a testament to this rich tradition. The museum showcases a vast collection of ceramics, ranging from ancient pottery to contemporary works. Visitors can learn about the history and techniques of ceramic production in the region, as well as admire the intricate designs and vibrant colors that characterize Vietri ceramics. The museum also features exhibits on the cultural and artistic heritage of the Amalfi Coast, making it a fascinating destination for art lovers and history enthusiasts.

In the hillside village of Scala, the Monastery of the Most Holy Redeemer is a historical site with deep religious significance. The monastery, founded in the 10th century, has been a center of spiritual life and education for centuries. The complex includes a church, cloisters, and gardens, all of which reflect the monastery's long and storied history. Visitors can explore the beautifully preserved buildings and learn about the lives of the monks who have lived and worked there over the centuries. The monastery's serene setting and rich history make it a unique and meaningful destination on the Amalfi Coast.

In conclusion, the Amalfi Coast is home to a wealth of historical sites and museums that offer invaluable insights into the region's rich cultural heritage. From ancient Roman villas and medieval cathedrals to museums dedicated to maritime history and traditional crafts, these attractions provide a deep and engaging exploration of the Amalfi Coast's past. By visiting these historical sites and museums, tourists can gain a greater understanding and appreciation of the region's history, art, and culture, ensuring a memorable and enriching experience.

Natural Wonders: Beaches, Grottos, and Hiking Trails

The Amalfi Coast is a destination of unparalleled natural beauty, known for its dramatic cliffs, picturesque villages, and the deep blue waters of the Mediterranean Sea. Among its many attractions, the region's natural wonders stand out as some of the most captivating and unforgettable experiences for tourists. From stunning beaches and mystical grottos to scenic hiking trails, the Amalfi Coast offers a wealth of opportunities to connect with nature and explore its breathtaking landscapes. This detailed guide will provide an in-depth look at these natural wonders, ensuring that visitors have all the information they need to make the most of their trip.

One of the most appealing aspects of the Amalfi Coast is its beautiful beaches. While some of the more popular beaches can be crowded, there are many hidden gems that offer a more peaceful and intimate experience. Spiaggia Grande in Positano is one of the largest and most well-known beaches on the coast. Its pebbled shoreline, clear waters, and stunning views of the colorful houses cascading down the cliffs make it a favorite among visitors. The beach is lined with beach clubs, restaurants, and shops, providing all the amenities needed for a relaxing day by the sea.

For those seeking a quieter and more secluded beach experience, Fornillo Beach, also in Positano, is a perfect choice. Accessible by a short walk from Spiaggia Grande, Fornillo Beach offers a more tranquil setting with fewer crowds. The beach is surrounded by lush vegetation and has a more laid-back atmosphere, making it an ideal spot for sunbathing and swimming. There are several beach clubs where visitors can rent sunbeds and umbrellas and enjoy refreshments throughout the day.

Another hidden gem is the Marina di Praia in Praiano, a small beach nestled between towering cliffs. This beach is known for its crystal-clear waters and charming fishing village ambiance. It is a great spot for swimming, snorkeling, and enjoying the peaceful surroundings. The beach is also home to several excellent seafood restaurants where visitors can savor fresh, local dishes while taking in the stunning views.

Further along the coast, the beach of Atrani is a true hidden treasure. Atrani is one of the smallest towns on the Amalfi Coast, and its beach reflects the town's intimate charm. The beach is situated at the mouth of a valley, with steep cliffs and terraced houses providing a dramatic backdrop. The calm waters and relaxed atmosphere make it a favorite among families and those looking for a quiet retreat. Atrani's beach is also conveniently located near the town's main square, where visitors can explore charming streets and historic buildings.

One of the most unique natural wonders of the Amalfi Coast is the Grotta dello Smeraldo, or the Emerald Grotto. Located near Conca dei Marini, this sea cave is renowned for its mesmerizing emerald-green waters, created by sunlight filtering through an underwater opening. Visitors can explore the grotto by boat, gliding through the luminous waters and admiring the stalactites and stalagmites that adorn the cave's interior. The Grotta dello Smeraldo is a magical experience that should not be missed.

Another fascinating grotto is the Grotta di Suppraiano, located in the town of Praiano. This lesser-known cave offers a more secluded and intimate experience compared to the Emerald Grotto. The cave can be reached by boat or by swimming from the nearby beach. Inside, visitors can marvel at the impressive rock formations and the shimmering blue waters that reflect the sunlight. The Grotta di Suppraiano is a hidden gem that provides a sense of adventure and discovery.

For those who enjoy hiking, the Amalfi Coast offers some of the most scenic trails in Italy. The Path of the Gods, or Sentiero degli Dei, is perhaps the most famous and spectacular hiking trail in the region. This trail runs from the village of Bomerano in Agerola to Nocelle, a hamlet above Positano. The Path of the Gods offers breathtaking views of the coastline, the sea, and the surrounding mountains. The trail is well-marked and suitable for hikers of all levels, making it a must-do for nature lovers and adventure seekers. Along the way, hikers pass through terraced vineyards, ancient ruins, and charming villages, providing a glimpse into the rich history and culture of the region.

Another fantastic hiking trail is the Valle delle Ferriere, a lush nature reserve located near Amalfi. This trail takes hikers through a verdant valley filled with waterfalls, rare plants, and ancient ruins. The trail follows the course of the Canneto River, passing through dense forests and alongside cascading streams. The Valle delle Ferriere is a haven for nature lovers, offering a tranquil escape from the bustling coastal towns. The trail also leads to the remains of old ironworks, providing insight into the region's industrial past.

The Sentiero dei Limoni, or Path of the Lemons, is another delightful hiking trail that takes visitors through the terraced lemon groves that are characteristic of the Amalfi Coast. This trail runs between the towns of Maiori and Minori, offering stunning views of the coastline and the lush lemon orchards. The scent of lemon blossoms fills the air as hikers traverse the path, providing a sensory experience that is uniquely Amalfi. The trail is relatively easy and suitable for all ages, making it a great option for families and casual hikers.

For a more challenging hike, the trail to the Monte Tre Calli offers spectacular panoramic views of the Amalfi Coast and the Bay of Naples. This trail starts in the village of Bomerano and ascends to the summit of Monte Tre Calli, providing a strenuous but rewarding hike. The trail passes through rugged terrain, pine forests, and rocky outcrops, culminating in breathtaking views from the summit. On clear days, hikers can see as far as the island of Capri and the distant mountains of Calabria.

In addition to its beaches, grottos, and hiking trails, the Amalfi Coast is home to several natural reserves and parks that showcase the region's diverse flora and fauna. The Monti Lattari Regional Park encompasses a large portion of the Amalfi Coast's mountainous interior, offering numerous hiking and biking trails that explore its rugged landscapes. The park is home to a wide variety of plant and animal species, including rare orchids, wild boar, and peregrine falcons. The park's trails provide opportunities for birdwatching, nature photography, and enjoying the pristine beauty of the Amalfi Coast's natural environment.

The Amalfi Coast is a treasure trove of natural wonders, from its stunning beaches and mystical grottos to its scenic hiking trails and lush nature reserves. These natural attractions offer visitors the chance to connect with the region's breathtaking landscapes and explore its diverse ecosystems. Whether you are seeking a peaceful retreat on a secluded beach, an adventurous hike through rugged terrain, or a magical boat trip through a glowing grotto, the Amalfi Coast has something to offer every nature lover. By immersing yourself in the natural beauty of this remarkable region, you can create unforgettable memories and gain a deeper appreciation for the Amalfi Coast's unique and enchanting environment.

Scenic Drives and Lookout Points

The Amalfi Coast, with its dramatic cliffs, azure waters, and charming towns, offers some of the most scenic drives and lookout points in Italy. Exploring this region by car allows visitors to take in the breathtaking views at their own pace, stopping at various points of interest along the way. The winding coastal roads and panoramic vistas make for an unforgettable driving experience.

One of the most famous and picturesque drives on the Amalfi Coast is the SS163, also known as the Amalfi Drive. This road stretches from Sorrento to Salerno, winding along the coastline and offering stunning views at every turn. The Amalfi Drive is renowned for its hairpin bends, narrow lanes, and sheer drops, making it both thrilling and awe-inspiring. The drive takes you through several iconic towns, including Positano, Amalfi, and Ravello, each with its own unique charm and attractions.

Starting from Sorrento, the drive along the SS163 begins with a gradual ascent, offering glimpses of the Bay of Naples and Mount Vesuvius in the distance. As you continue along the road, the landscape becomes more rugged, with cliffs plunging into the sea and terraced vineyards clinging to the hillsides. One of the first major stops is Positano, a picturesque town known for its pastel-colored houses cascading down the cliffs. The viewpoint from the SS163 just before entering Positano provides a stunning panorama of the town and the surrounding coastline, making it a popular spot for photographs.

Continuing along the Amalfi Drive, the next major town is Praiano. This quieter and less touristy town offers several scenic lookout points where visitors can enjoy views of the coastline and the distant island of Capri. The Marina di Praia, a small beach nestled between cliffs, is particularly picturesque and worth a stop. The drive from Praiano to Amalfi is especially scenic, with the road hugging the cliffs and offering uninterrupted views of the Mediterranean Sea.

Amalfi, one of the main towns on the coast, is a must-visit stop along the drive. The town's historic center, with its narrow streets and bustling piazza, is a delight to explore. The viewpoint from the road above Amalfi offers a magnificent view of the town and its iconic cathedral, with the mountains rising steeply behind. Continuing from Amalfi, the road climbs steeply to Ravello, a hilltop town known for its stunning gardens and panoramic views. The viewpoints from Villa Rufolo and Villa Cimbrone in Ravello are among the most beautiful on the coast, offering sweeping vistas of the coastline and the sea.

As you continue along the SS163, the road winds through several smaller towns, each with its own unique charm. One of these is Atrani, a tiny village nestled in a narrow valley. The viewpoint from the road above Atrani offers a beautiful view of the village's cluster of whitewashed houses, with the sea in the background. Further along, the town of Minori offers another picturesque stop, with its sandy beach and historic Roman villa.

Another scenic drive worth exploring is the road from Amalfi to Agerola. This road, known as the SP366, climbs steeply from the coast, offering spectacular views of the Amalfi Coast from above. The drive takes you through lush forests and terraced vineyards, with several lookout points along the way where you can stop and take in the views. Agerola, located high in the hills, is known for its hiking trails and beautiful landscapes. The viewpoint from the village offers a stunning panorama of the coastline, with the towns of Amalfi and Ravello visible in the distance.

For those looking for a more off-the-beaten-path drive, the road to the village of Scala offers a tranquil and scenic experience. This road winds through the hills above Amalfi, passing through forests and vineyards. Scala is one of the oldest towns on the Amalfi Coast, and its historic center is a delight to explore. The viewpoint from the road above Scala offers a beautiful view of the town and the surrounding countryside.

In addition to these scenic drives, there are several lookout points along the Amalfi Coast that are worth a visit. One of the most famous is the Terrace of Infinity at Villa Cimbrone in Ravello. This terrace offers one of the most breathtaking views on the Amalfi Coast, with its marble busts and panoramic vistas of the coastline and the Mediterranean Sea. The view from the Terrace of Infinity is truly awe-inspiring, providing a sense of boundless beauty and tranquility.

Another noteworthy lookout point is the viewpoint at Punta Campanella, located at the tip of the Sorrento Peninsula. This viewpoint offers a stunning view of the Amalfi Coast, the Bay of Naples, and the island of Capri. The drive to Punta Campanella is scenic in itself, with the road winding through olive groves and lemon orchards. The viewpoint is a popular spot for watching the sunset, with the sea and sky bathed in golden light.

The Sentiero degli Dei, or Path of the Gods, also offers several scenic lookout points along its route. This hiking trail runs from Bomerano to Nocelle, offering spectacular views of the Amalfi Coast and the surrounding mountains. The viewpoints along the trail provide a different perspective of the coastline, with the towns of Positano and Praiano visible in the distance. The trail is well-marked and suitable for hikers of all levels, making it a must-do for nature lovers and adventure seekers.

For those interested in exploring the coastline by sea, the Amalfi Coast offers several boat tours that provide a unique perspective of the region's natural beauty. These tours often include stops at secluded beaches and grottos, allowing visitors to experience the coastline from a different angle. The viewpoint from the sea offers a stunning panorama of the cliffs and towns that make up the Amalfi Coast, providing a memorable and immersive experience.

The Amalfi Coast offers some of the most scenic drives and lookout points in Italy, providing visitors with unforgettable views of the region's dramatic landscapes and charming towns. Whether you are exploring the Amalfi Drive, winding through the hills above Amalfi, or hiking along the Path of the Gods, the Amalfi Coast's natural beauty is sure to leave a lasting impression. By taking the time to explore these scenic drives and lookout points, you can gain a deeper appreciation for the unique and enchanting environment of the Amalfi Coast.

CHAPTER 6

Experiencing the Local Culture

Festivals and Events

The Amalfi Coast is not only renowned for its breathtaking landscapes and historic towns but also for its rich cultural heritage, which is vibrantly showcased through a variety of festivals and events throughout the year. These celebrations, deeply rooted in tradition, offer visitors a unique opportunity to experience the local culture, history, and community spirit. From music festivals and religious processions to food fairs and historical reenactments, the Amalfi Coast's festivals and events provide a fascinating glimpse into the region's way of life.

One of the most famous and enduring festivals on the Amalfi Coast is the Ravello Festival. Held annually in the town of Ravello, this festival is a celebration of music and the arts, attracting artists and audiences from around the world. The Ravello Festival was founded in 1953 in honor of the composer Richard Wagner, who found inspiration in the beauty of Villa Rufolo. The festival features a diverse program of classical music, opera, ballet, and jazz performances, often held in the stunning gardens of Villa Rufolo and other picturesque venues around Ravello. The festival runs from June to September, offering a unique cultural experience set against the backdrop of the Amalfi Coast's scenic beauty.

Another significant event is the Amalfi Coast Music & Arts Festival, which takes place in various towns along the coast, including Amalfi, Positano, and Maiori. This international festival brings together musicians, artists, and students for a series of concerts, exhibitions, and workshops. The festival aims to promote cultural exchange and artistic collaboration, offering a platform for emerging talents and established artists alike. Visitors can enjoy a wide range of performances, from classical and contemporary music to visual arts and theater, all set in the charming and historic surroundings of the Amalfi Coast.

Religious festivals play a central role in the cultural life of the Amalfi Coast, with many towns celebrating their patron saints with elaborate processions, masses, and communal feasts. One of the most important religious festivals is the Feast of St. Andrew (Festa di Sant'Andrea), held in Amalfi on June 27th and November 30th. St. Andrew is the patron saint of Amalfi, and his relics are housed in the town's cathedral. The festival features a solemn procession through the streets of Amalfi, where the statue of St. Andrew is carried by local fishermen and townspeople. The procession is accompanied by music, prayers, and fireworks, creating a vibrant and festive atmosphere. The event culminates with a special mass in the cathedral and a communal celebration in the town's main square.

In Positano, the Feast of Our Lady of the Assumption (Festa della Madonna Assunta) is celebrated on August 15th. This festival honors the town's patron saint, and the highlight is a grand procession that winds through the streets of Positano to the Church of Santa Maria Assunta. The procession is a colorful and joyous event, with participants dressed in traditional costumes, carrying banners and candles. The festival also includes music, dancing, and spectacular fireworks display over the sea, making it a memorable experience for both locals and visitors.

Maiori hosts the Feast of Santa Maria a Mare on August 15th, another significant religious festival on the Amalfi Coast. The festival celebrates the town's patron saint, and the main event is a procession that carries the statue of Santa Maria a Mare from the Church of Santa Maria a Mare to the sea. The procession is accompanied by prayers, hymns, and the ringing of church bells. The festival also includes a fireworks display, a communal feast, and various cultural and entertainment events, reflecting the strong sense of community and tradition in Maiori.

The Historical Regatta of the Ancient Maritime Republics (Regata delle Antiche Repubbliche Marinare) is a unique and exciting event that takes place every four years in Amalfi. This historical reenactment commemorates the maritime prowess and rivalry of the four ancient Italian maritime republics: Amalfi, Genoa, Pisa, and Venice. The regatta features a rowing race in traditional boats, each representing one of the republics, with crews dressed in historical costumes. The event also includes a colorful parade with participants in medieval attire, flag throwers, and musicians, creating a vibrant and festive atmosphere. The Historical Regatta is a captivating spectacle that brings the rich maritime history of Amalfi to life.

The Lemon Festival (Sagra del Limone) in Minori is a delightful celebration of one of the Amalfi Coast's most iconic products: the lemon. Held in July, the festival showcases the region's famous lemons, known for their large size and intense flavor. The event includes tastings of lemon-based products such as limoncello, lemon cake, and lemon ice cream. Visitors can also enjoy cooking demonstrations, live music, and folk dancing, all set in the charming town of Minori. The Lemon Festival is a wonderful opportunity to experience the culinary traditions and local flavors of the Amalfi Coast.

Another food-related event is the Anchovy Festival (Sagra delle Alici) in Cetara, a small fishing village known for its anchovy fishing and production of colatura di alici, a traditional anchovy sauce. The festival, held in July, celebrates Cetara's anchovy heritage with tastings of anchovy-based dishes, cooking demonstrations, and fishing demonstrations. The event also features live music, dancing, and a festive atmosphere, offering visitors a taste of the local culture and cuisine.

The GustaMinori Festival in Minori is a celebration of local food, wine, and culture. Held in September, the festival features food and wine tastings, cooking demonstrations, and cultural performances. Visitors can sample a wide range of local dishes, including seafood, pasta, and pastries, all made with fresh, local ingredients. The festival also includes live music, theater performances, and art exhibitions, making it a vibrant and engaging event that showcases the rich cultural heritage of Minori.

In Praiano, the Luminaria di San Domenico is a unique and visually stunning festival held in August. The festival honors St. Dominic, the patron saint of Praiano, with a series of events that include processions, masses, and communal feasts. The highlight of the festival is the illumination of the town with thousands of candles, creating a magical and ethereal atmosphere. The streets, squares, and houses of Praiano are adorned with candles and lanterns, and the event also includes fireworks and live music. The Luminaria di San Domenico is a truly enchanting experience that showcases the beauty and community spirit of Praiano.

In conclusion, the Amalfi Coast is home to a wide variety of festivals and events that celebrate the region's rich cultural heritage, religious traditions, and local flavors. From the world-renowned Ravello Festival and the Historical Regatta of the Ancient Maritime Republics to the Lemon Festival in Minori and the Anchovy Festival in Cetara, these events offer visitors a unique and immersive experience of the

Amalfi Coast. By participating in these festivals and events, tourists can gain a deeper understanding and appreciation of the region's history, culture, and community, ensuring a memorable and enriching visit to this stunning part of Italy.

Traditional Music and Dance

The Amalfi Coast, known for its stunning landscapes, historical landmarks, and vibrant culture, is also rich in traditional music and dance. These cultural expressions are deeply rooted in the history and daily life of the region, reflecting the joys, sorrows, and rhythms of the coastal communities. Traditional music and dance on the Amalfi Coast offer visitors a captivating glimpse into the local heritage, providing a deeper understanding of the area's cultural identity.

One of the most iconic and well-loved forms of traditional music on the Amalfi Coast is the tarantella. The tarantella is a lively and rhythmic folk dance that is accompanied by music featuring guitars, mandolins, tambourines, and castanets. The origins of the tarantella are steeped in legend and folklore. It is said to have originated as a dance to cure the bite of the tarantula spider, with the fast-paced movements helping to sweat out the poison. Over time, the tarantella evolved into a social and celebratory dance, performed at weddings, festivals, and other communal gatherings.

The tarantella is characterized by its rapid tempo and lively, infectious rhythms. Dancers typically perform in pairs or groups, with quick, intricate footwork and exuberant spins. The music often features a repeating melody, with variations and improvisations that keep the energy high and the dancers engaged. The tarantella is not only a dance but also a symbol of joy, celebration, and community spirit on the Amalfi Coast.

Another important aspect of traditional music on the Amalfi Coast is the use of the tammorra, a large frame drum with jingles that is played with the hands. The tammorra is a central instrument in many traditional music ensembles and is often used to accompany dances like the tarantella. The rhythmic patterns played on the tammorra are complex and varied, adding a rich and dynamic layer to the music. The drum's deep, resonant sound can be heard in many traditional songs and performances, providing a powerful and rhythmic foundation for the melodies and harmonies.

The canzone napoletana, or Neapolitan song, is another significant genre of traditional music that has influenced the Amalfi Coast. These songs are known for their beautiful melodies, poetic lyrics, and expressive vocal styles. The canzone napoletana often tells stories of love, longing, and everyday life, capturing the emotions and experiences of the people of the region. Famous examples of this genre include "O Sole Mio," "Funiculì Funiculà," and "Santa Lucia." These songs are performed by solo singers or small ensembles, accompanied by instruments such as the guitar, mandolin, and accordion. The canzone napoletana has a timeless quality, and its melodies continue to resonate with both locals and visitors.

In addition to the tarantella and the canzone napoletana, the Amalfi Coast is home to a variety of other traditional dances and music forms that reflect the region's diverse cultural influences. The tammurriata, for example, is a traditional dance that is closely associated with the tammorra drum. The dance is performed in a circular formation, with dancers moving in sync with the rhythm of the drum. The movements are expressive and often include gestures that mimic daily activities or tell a story. The tammurriata is a dance of community and celebration, bringing people together in a shared experience of music and movement.

The pastoral music of the Amalfi Coast is another important tradition, particularly in the rural and mountainous areas of the region. This music is often played on traditional instruments such as the zampogna (a type of bagpipe), the ciaramella (a double-reed woodwind instrument), and the fischiotto (a type of whistle). Pastoral music is typically performed during festivals, religious celebrations, and other communal gatherings. The melodies and rhythms are often simple and repetitive, creating a soothing and meditative atmosphere. This music reflects the close relationship between the people and the land, celebrating the natural beauty and agricultural heritage of the region.

One of the most vibrant and lively expressions of traditional music and dance on the Amalfi Coast can be experienced during the region's many festivals and celebrations. These events often feature performances by local musicians and dance groups, showcasing the rich cultural heritage of the area. The Feast of St. Andrew in Amalfi, for example, includes processions, music, and dancing, with traditional tunes and dances like the tarantella playing a central role. Similarly, the Luminaria di San Domenico in Praiano features music and dance performances that highlight the region's cultural traditions.

Another important cultural event is the Ravello Festival, which, while primarily focused on classical music and the arts, often includes performances of traditional music and dance. The festival provides a platform for both local and international artists, creating a vibrant and dynamic cultural exchange. Visitors to the festival can enjoy a diverse program that includes traditional Neapolitan songs, folk dances, and contemporary interpretations of classic pieces.

In addition to these public performances, traditional music and dance are also an integral part of private celebrations and family gatherings on the Amalfi Coast. Weddings, baptisms, and other significant life events often feature traditional music and dance, creating a festive and joyful atmosphere. These traditions are passed down through generations, preserving the cultural heritage of the region and ensuring that it remains a vital and living part of community life.

Learning about and experiencing traditional music and dance on the Amalfi Coast offers visitors a deeper understanding of the region's cultural identity. These art forms are more than just entertainment; they are a reflection of the history, values, and daily life of the local communities. The melodies and rhythms tell stories of love, hardship, joy, and celebration, connecting the past with the present and fostering a sense of continuity and belonging.

For those interested in exploring traditional music and dance more deeply, there are opportunities to take part in workshops and classes offered by local cultural organizations and music schools. These programs provide hands-on experience and instruction in playing traditional instruments, singing, and dancing, allowing visitors to engage with the culture in a meaningful and immersive way. Whether you are a seasoned musician or a complete beginner, these workshops offer a unique and enriching way to connect with the cultural heritage of the Amalfi Coast.

Artisan Shops and Markets

The Amalfi Coast, with its stunning scenery and rich cultural heritage, is also a treasure trove for those interested in artisanal crafts and local markets. The region boasts a long tradition of craftsmanship, with artisans creating everything from ceramics and textiles to food products and leather goods. Exploring the artisan shops and markets along the

Amalfi Coast offers a unique opportunity to discover the local culture and take home a piece of its heritage. This detailed guide will provide an in-depth look at the various artisan shops and markets, ensuring that visitors have a comprehensive understanding of what to expect and where to go.

One of the most renowned forms of craftsmanship on the Amalfi Coast is ceramics. The town of Vietri sul Mare is particularly famous for its vibrant ceramics, known as "ceramica vietrese." These ceramics are characterized by their bright colors and intricate designs, often featuring local motifs such as lemons, fish, and coastal landscapes. The tradition of ceramics in Vietri sul Mare dates back to the 15th century, and today, the town is home to numerous workshops and boutiques where artisans continue to create these beautiful pieces. Visitors can find a wide range of items, from decorative plates and vases to tiles and kitchenware. Some of the most notable shops include Ceramica Artistica Solimene, which is housed in a distinctive circular building designed by the architect Paolo Soleri, and Ceramica Pinto, known for its high-quality handcrafted ceramics.

Another important craft in the region is paper-making, which has been practiced in Amalfi since the 12th century. Amalfi paper, or "carta di Amalfi," is renowned for its high quality and distinctive texture. Made from cotton and linen fibers, this handmade paper is often used for writing, printing, and bookbinding. Visitors can learn about the traditional paper-making process at the Paper Museum (Museo della Carta) in Amalfi, which is housed in a historic paper mill. The museum offers guided tours and demonstrations, providing insight into the techniques and history of this ancient craft. In addition to the museum, there are several shops in Amalfi where visitors can purchase beautiful stationery, journals, and other paper products made from Amalfi paper.

The Amalfi Coast is also known for its textiles, particularly hand-loomed fabrics and intricate embroidery. In the town of Positano, visitors can find shops that specialize in linen clothing and accessories, reflecting the town's long tradition of textile production. These shops offer a variety of handmade items, including dresses, shirts, scarves, and bags, all crafted from high-quality natural fibers. The vibrant colors and unique designs make these textiles a perfect souvenir or gift. One notable shop is Emporio Le Sirenuse, which offers a range of luxury clothing and home goods inspired by the Amalfi Coast's heritage and aesthetics.

Food products are another highlight of the artisan shops and markets on the Amalfi Coast. The region is famous for its lemons, which are used to make a variety of delicious products, including limoncello, a popular lemon liqueur. Visitors can find limoncello in many shops and markets, often packaged in beautifully decorated bottles. Some shops, such as Limonoro in Amalfi, offer tastings and tours, allowing visitors to learn about the production process and sample different varieties of limoncello. In addition to limoncello, the Amalfi Coast is known for its lemon-infused olive oil, honey, and pastries, all of which make excellent gifts and souvenirs.

The town of Minori is famous for its pasta, particularly a type known as "ndunderi," which dates back to Roman times. Local shops and markets offer a variety of handmade pasta, as well as other traditional food products such as anchovy sauce (colatura di alici) from Cetara, and fig jam from the hills above Amalfi. These artisanal food products provide a taste of the region's culinary heritage and are a delight for food lovers.

Leather goods are another specialty of the Amalfi Coast, with artisans creating high-quality items such as sandals, bags, and belts. In Positano, visitors can find shops that specialize in handmade leather sandals, a tradition that dates back to the 1960s. These sandals are often customized to fit the customer's feet and can be embellished with a variety of decorative elements. Some of the most well-known shops include Safari Sandals and Nana Positano, both of which offer a range of beautifully crafted leather goods.

Markets are an integral part of the cultural and social life on the Amalfi Coast, providing a lively and vibrant atmosphere where locals and visitors can shop for fresh produce, artisanal products, and handmade crafts. The markets are held on specific days in different towns, each offering a unique selection of goods. The market in Amalfi, held on Wednesdays, is one of the largest and most diverse, featuring stalls selling everything from fresh fruit and vegetables to clothing and ceramics. The market in Maiori, held on Fridays, is another popular destination, offering a wide range of local products and crafts.

In addition to these weekly markets, there are also seasonal and specialty markets that highlight specific products and traditions. The Christmas markets, held in various towns along the coast, offer a festive atmosphere with stalls selling holiday decorations, gifts, and traditional food and drink. These markets provide a wonderful opportunity to experience the local culture and traditions during the holiday season.

The artisans on the Amalfi Coast are known for their skill and creativity, and many of them are happy to share their knowledge and techniques with visitors. Some workshops and studios offer classes and demonstrations, allowing visitors to learn about the traditional crafts and even try their hand at making their own pieces. These experiences provide a deeper connection to the local culture and a greater appreciation for the craftsmanship that goes into creating these beautiful items.

The artisan shops and markets on the Amalfi Coast offer a rich and diverse array of products that reflect the region's cultural heritage and artistic traditions. From vibrant ceramics and handmade paper to luxurious textiles and delicious food products, there is something for everyone to discover and enjoy. By exploring these shops and markets, visitors can gain a deeper understanding of the local culture, support the artisans who keep these traditions alive, and take home unique and meaningful souvenirs from their time on the Amalfi Coast. Whether you are looking for a special gift, a taste of the local cuisine, or a beautifully crafted piece of art, the artisan shops and markets of the Amalfi Coast provide a wealth of opportunities to experience the region's rich cultural heritage.

Local Crafts and Souvenirs

The Amalfi Coast, with its breathtaking landscapes, historic towns, and rich cultural heritage, is also a haven for local crafts and souvenirs. The region's long-standing tradition of craftsmanship means that visitors can find a variety of unique and high-quality items that reflect the area's history, culture, and artistic spirit. From vibrant ceramics and intricate textiles to delicious food products and beautifully crafted leather goods, the Amalfi Coast offers an array of souvenirs that are perfect for remembering your visit or sharing a piece of this stunning region with loved ones.

One of the most iconic and sought-after crafts on the Amalfi Coast is ceramics. The town of Vietri sul Mare is especially famous for its vibrant and colorful ceramics, known as "ceramica vietrese." These ceramics are characterized by their bright colors, intricate designs, and the use of traditional motifs such as lemons, fish, and coastal landscapes. The tradition of ceramics in Vietri sul Mare dates back to the 15th century, and today, the town is home to numerous workshops and boutiques where skilled artisans continue to create beautiful pieces. Visitors can find a wide range of items, from decorative plates and vases to tiles and kitchenware. Each piece is often hand-painted, making it a unique work of art. Some of the most renowned shops include Ceramica Artistica Solimene and Ceramica Pinto, both of which offer an extensive selection of handcrafted ceramics.

Another important craft in the region is paper-making, which has been practiced in Amalfi since the 12th century. Amalfi paper, or "carta di Amalfi," is renowned for its high quality and distinctive texture. Made from cotton and linen fibers, this handmade paper is often used for writing, printing, and bookbinding. Visitors can learn about the traditional paper-making process at the Paper Museum (Museo della Carta) in Amalfi, which is housed in a historic paper mill. The museum offers guided tours and demonstrations, providing insight into the techniques and history of this ancient craft. In addition to the museum, there are several shops in Amalfi where visitors can purchase beautiful stationery, journals, and other paper products made from Amalfi paper. These items make for elegant and unique souvenirs that capture the essence of the region's artisanal heritage.

Textiles are another significant craft on the Amalfi Coast, with a particular emphasis on hand-loomed fabrics and intricate embroidery. In the town of Positano, visitors can find shops that specialize in linen clothing and accessories, reflecting the town's long tradition of textile production. These shops offer a variety of handmade items, including dresses, shirts, scarves, and bags, all crafted from high-quality natural fibers. The vibrant colors and unique designs make these textiles a perfect souvenir or gift. One notable shop is Emporio Le Sirenuse, which offers a range of luxury clothing and home goods inspired by the Amalfi Coast's heritage and aesthetics.

Food products are also a highlight of the local crafts and souvenirs on the Amalfi Coast. The region is famous for its lemons, which are used to make a variety of delicious products, including limoncello, a popular lemon liqueur. Visitors can find limoncello in many shops and markets, often packaged in beautifully decorated bottles. Some shops, such as Limonoro in Amalfi, offer tastings and tours, allowing visitors to learn about the production process and sample different varieties of limoncello. In addition to limoncello, the Amalfi Coast is known for its lemon-infused olive oil, honey, and pastries, all of which make excellent gifts and souvenirs.

The town of Minori is famous for its pasta, particularly a type known as "ndunderi," which dates back to Roman times. Local shops and markets offer a variety of handmade pasta, as well as other traditional food products such as anchovy sauce (colatura di alici) from Cetara, and fig jam from the hills above Amalfi. These artisanal food products provide a taste of the region's culinary heritage and are a delight for food lovers. Visitors can also find a selection of local wines, olive oils, and balsamic vinegars, which are produced in the surrounding countryside and make for delicious and memorable souvenirs.

Leather goods are another specialty of the Amalfi Coast, with artisans creating high-quality items such as sandals, bags, and belts. In Positano, visitors can find shops that specialize in handmade leather sandals, a tradition that dates back to the 1960s. These sandals are often customized to fit the customer's feet and can be embellished with a variety of decorative elements. Some of the most well-known shops include Safari Sandals and Nana Positano, both of which offer a range of beautifully crafted leather goods. These items are not only stylish and durable but also reflect the region's artisanal expertise.

Jewelry is another popular souvenir from the Amalfi Coast, with many shops offering handcrafted pieces that incorporate local materials and traditional designs. Coral and cameos are particularly prominent, with artisans creating intricate necklaces, bracelets, and earrings that capture the beauty of the sea and the history of the region. Visitors can find a variety of jewelry shops in towns like Amalfi and Positano, where skilled craftsmen continue to produce exquisite pieces that make for timeless and meaningful souvenirs.

In addition to individual artisan shops, the markets on the Amalfi Coast offer a vibrant and lively atmosphere where visitors can shop for a wide range of local crafts and souvenirs. The markets are held on specific days in different towns, each offering a unique selection of goods. The market in Amalfi, held on Wednesdays, is one of the largest and most diverse, featuring stalls selling everything from fresh fruit and vegetables to clothing and ceramics. The market in Maiori, held on Fridays, is another popular destination, offering a wide range of local products and crafts. These markets provide an excellent opportunity to explore the region's artisanal offerings and find unique and high-quality souvenirs.

The artisans on the Amalfi Coast are known for their skill and creativity, and many of them are happy to share their knowledge and techniques with visitors. Some workshops and studios offer classes and demonstrations, allowing visitors to learn about the traditional crafts and even try their hand at making their own pieces. These experiences provide a deeper connection to the local culture and a greater appreciation for the craftsmanship that goes into creating these beautiful items. Whether you are interested in ceramics, textiles, paper-making, or any other craft, there are opportunities to engage with the artisans and gain insight into their work.

The local crafts and souvenirs on the Amalfi Coast offer a rich and diverse array of products that reflect the region's cultural heritage and artistic traditions. From vibrant ceramics and handmade paper to luxurious textiles and delicious food products, there is something for everyone to discover and enjoy. By exploring the artisan shops and markets, visitors can gain a deeper understanding of the local culture, support the artisans who keep these traditions alive, and take home unique and meaningful souvenirs from their time on the Amalfi Coast. Whether you are looking for a special gift, a taste of the local cuisine, or a beautifully crafted piece of art, the local crafts and souvenirs of the Amalfi Coast provide a wealth of opportunities to experience the region's rich cultural heritage.

Language and Useful Phrases

The Amalfi Coast is a region of Italy known for its stunning coastal landscapes, charming towns, and rich cultural heritage. While many tourists visit the area, having a basic understanding of the Italian language and some useful phrases can greatly enhance your experience and interactions with locals. Italian is the official language of the region, and although English is widely understood in tourist areas, speaking even a little Italian can show respect for the local culture and make your trip more enjoyable.

Italian is a Romance language, closely related to Latin, and shares similarities with other Romance languages such as

Spanish, French, and Portuguese. It is known for its melodic and rhythmic quality, which makes it pleasant to speak and listen to. The Italian alphabet consists of 21 letters, as it does not include the letters j, k, w, x, and y, which are only used in foreign words. Pronunciation in Italian is relatively straightforward, as words are pronounced as they are written, with each letter having a consistent sound.

When visiting the Amalfi Coast, knowing a few basic Italian phrases can go a long way in making your interactions with locals smoother and more pleasant. Here are some essential greetings and polite expressions:

1. Buongiorno (bwon-JOR-noh) – Good morning
2. Buonasera (bwoh-nah-SEH-rah) – Good evening
3. Ciao (chow) – Hello/Goodbye (informal)
4. Arrivederci (ah-ree-veh-DER-chee) – Goodbye (formal)
5. Per favore (pehr fah-VOH-reh) – Please
6. Grazie (GRAH-tsyeh) – Thank you
7. Prego (PREH-goh) – You're welcome
8. Scusi (SKOO-zee) – Excuse me (formal)
9. Mi scusi (mee SKOO-zee) – Excuse me (to get attention)
10. Sì (see) – Yes
11. No (noh) – No

These basic phrases will help you with everyday interactions, such as greeting people, asking for help, and showing politeness. Italians appreciate it when visitors make an effort to speak their language, and using these phrases can create a positive impression.

When dining out or shopping, knowing some useful phrases specific to these situations can be very helpful. Here are some phrases that can enhance your experience in restaurants and cafes:

1. Un tavolo per due, per favore (oon TAH-voh-loh pehr doo-eh, pehr fah-VOH-reh) – A table for two, please
2. Il menù, per favore (eel meh-NOO, pehr fah-VOH-reh) – The menu, please
3. Che cosa mi consiglia? (keh KOH-zah mee kohn-SEEL-yah) – What do you recommend?
4. Vorrei ordinare… (vohr-REY or-dee-NAH-reh) – I would like to order…
5. L'acqua, per favore (LAH-kwah, pehr fah-VOH-reh) – Water, please
6. Il conto, per favore (eel KOHN-toh, pehr fah-VOH-reh) – The bill, please
7. Posso avere…? (POHS-soh ah-VEH-reh…?) – Can I have…?
8. Senza glutine (SEHN-tsah GLOO-tee-neh) – Gluten-free
9. Vegetariano (veh-jeh-tah-ree-AH-noh) – Vegetarian

When shopping in local markets or stores, these phrases can come in handy:
1. Quanto costa? (KWAHN-toh KOH-stah?) – How much does it cost?

2. Mi piace (mee PYA-cheh) – I like it

3. Non mi piace (nohn mee PYA-cheh) – I don't like it

4. Posso vedere? (POHS-soh veh-DEH-reh?) – Can I see it?

5. C'è una taglia più grande/piccola? (cheh OO-nah TAH-lyah pyoo GRAHN-deh/PEEK-koh-lah?) – Is there a larger/smaller size?

6. Accettate carte di credito? (ah-cheh-TAH-teh KAHR-teh dee KREH-dee-toh?) – Do you accept credit cards?

In addition to these practical phrases, understanding some common Italian expressions can enhance your cultural experience. Italians often use idiomatic expressions that reflect their vibrant culture and way of life. For example:

1. In bocca al lupo (een BOHK-kah ahl LOO-poh) – Good luck (literally: in the wolf's mouth)

2. Crepi (KREH-pee) – Thank you (response to in bocca al lupo, literally: may the wolf die)

3. Avere le mani bucate (ah-VEH-reh leh MAH-nee boo-KAH-teh) – To be a big spender (literally: to have holes in one's hands)

4. Essere al settimo cielo (EH-sseh-reh ahl SEHT-tee-moh cheh-loh) – To be on cloud nine (literally: to be in the seventh heaven)

Understanding these expressions can provide deeper insights into the Italian way of thinking and communicating, making your interactions more meaningful.

For travelers who wish to dig deeper into the language, it can be helpful to familiarize yourself with some basic grammar and sentence structures. Italian sentences typically follow a subject-verb-object order, similar to English. For example, "Io mangio una pizza" means "I eat a pizza," where "Io" is the subject, "mangio" is the verb, and "una pizza" is the object.

Verbs in Italian are conjugated according to the subject and tense, which can be different from English. For example, the verb "mangiare" (to eat) is conjugated as follows in the present tense:
1. Io mangio – I eat
2. Tu mangi – You eat (singular, informal)
3. Lui/Lei mangia – He/She eats
4. Noi mangiamo – We eat
5. Voi mangiate – You eat (plural)
6. Loro mangiano – They eat

Nouns in Italian have gender (masculine or feminine) and number (singular or plural). For example, "il libro" (the book) is masculine singular, while "i libri" (the books) is masculine plural. Similarly, "la casa" (the house) is feminine singular, and "le case" (the houses) is feminine plural.

Adjectives in Italian agree in gender and number with the nouns they describe. For example, "un bel libro" (a beautiful book) and "una bella casa" (a beautiful house) demonstrate how the adjective "bello" changes to agree with the noun.

By understanding these basic grammatical rules, travelers can start to form their own sentences and better understand the structure of the language.

Learning some basic Italian phrases and understanding the language can greatly enhance your experience on the Amalfi Coast. It allows you to engage more deeply with the local culture, make connections with residents, and navigate your travels more smoothly. From simple greetings and polite expressions to practical phrases for dining and shopping, this guide provides a comprehensive overview to help you communicate effectively. Additionally, delving into the structure and nuances of the language can enrich your understanding and appreciation of Italian culture, making your visit to the Amalfi Coast even more memorable and rewarding.

CHAPTER 7

CULINARY DELIGHTS

Best Restaurants and Eateries

The Amalfi Coast is renowned not only for its breathtaking landscapes and historic sites but also for its exceptional culinary offerings. The region boasts a rich culinary heritage, combining fresh local ingredients with traditional recipes passed down through generations. The result is a vibrant food scene that ranges from family-run trattorias to upscale Michelin-starred restaurants. Exploring the best restaurants and eateries on the Amalfi Coast is a journey through the flavors and aromas that define this stunning part of Italy.

One of the most celebrated dining experiences on the Amalfi Coast is found at La Caravella in Amalfi. This historic restaurant, established in 1959, has earned a Michelin star for its exceptional cuisine. La Caravella offers a menu that showcases the best of local seafood, fresh vegetables, and traditional recipes. Signature dishes include linguine with clams, risotto with Amalfi lemons, and fresh fish grilled to perfection. The restaurant's interior is adorned with beautiful ceramics and antiques, creating an elegant and intimate atmosphere. Dining at La Caravella is not just a meal but a journey through the culinary traditions of the region.

In the picturesque town of Positano, Ristorante La Sponda at Le Sirenuse Hotel is a must-visit for its breathtaking views and exquisite cuisine. Illuminated by hundreds of candles in the evening, La Sponda offers a romantic and magical dining experience. The menu, inspired by Mediterranean flavors, features dishes such as lobster with citrus fruits, ricotta-stuffed zucchini flowers, and homemade pasta with fresh seafood. The restaurant's terrace provides stunning views of Positano and the Mediterranean Sea, making it an ideal spot for a special occasion or a memorable evening out.

For a more casual yet equally delightful dining experience, Da Adolfo in Laurito Beach near Positano is a hidden gem. Accessible only by boat, this beachfront trattoria offers a relaxed atmosphere and delicious seafood. Guests can enjoy fresh grilled fish, mussels, and the restaurant's famous mozzarella grilled on lemon leaves. The rustic setting, with tables right on the beach, makes for a unique and unforgettable meal. Da Adolfo is perfect for those looking to enjoy the simple pleasures of fresh, local food in a beautiful, natural setting.

In the charming town of Ravello, Ristorante Rossellinis at Palazzo Avino is another Michelin-starred gem. The restaurant offers an elegant dining experience with a menu that blends traditional Italian cuisine with modern culinary techniques. Dishes such as beef fillet with truffle sauce, ravioli filled with ricotta and lemon, and lobster with artichokes are presented with artistic flair. The terrace at

Rossellinis provides panoramic views of the coastline, adding to the restaurant's allure. The impeccable service and attention to detail make dining at Rossellinis a truly special experience.

Another standout in Ravello is Cumpa' Cosimo, a family-run trattoria known for its hearty, home-cooked meals. The restaurant has been serving traditional Italian dishes for over 80 years, with recipes passed down through generations. The menu includes classics such as gnocchi alla sorrentina, spaghetti alle vongole, and veal scaloppine. The warm and welcoming atmosphere, combined with the delicious food, makes Cumpa' Cosimo a favorite among locals and visitors alike.

In the town of Amalfi, Trattoria da Gemma is a beloved institution known for its traditional cuisine and warm hospitality. The restaurant's menu features a variety of local specialties, including seafood risotto, grilled fish, and the famous "cappuccino" dessert made with layers of coffee and chocolate mousse. The cozy interior and friendly service create a relaxed and inviting dining experience. Trattoria da Gemma is a great place to sample authentic Amalfi Coast cuisine in a comfortable and unpretentious setting.

For a unique and immersive dining experience, Il Refettorio at Monastero Santa Rosa in Conca dei Marini offers a blend of history, luxury, and culinary excellence. Housed in a former monastery, this Michelin-starred restaurant serves a menu inspired by the monastic tradition of simplicity and purity. Dishes such as rabbit with wild herbs, homemade pasta with truffles, and lemon-scented sea bass highlight the fresh, local ingredients and creative presentation. The restaurant's terrace offers breathtaking views of the coastline, providing a serene and memorable backdrop for an exceptional meal.

In the fishing village of Cetara, Ristorante Al Convento is renowned for its seafood dishes and traditional recipes. The restaurant's menu features a variety of fish and seafood, including anchovies, tuna, and squid, prepared in both classic and innovative ways. The "spaghetti alla colatura di alici," made with a traditional anchovy sauce, is a must-try. The rustic charm of the restaurant, combined with its focus on fresh, local ingredients, makes Al Convento a standout dining destination on the Amalfi Coast.

Another noteworthy eatery in Cetara is Ristorante San Pietro, known for its fresh seafood and beautiful seaside location. The restaurant's menu includes dishes such as spaghetti with sea urchins, grilled octopus, and fish carpaccio. The outdoor terrace, overlooking the marina, provides a perfect setting for enjoying a leisurely meal while taking in the picturesque views. Ristorante San Pietro offers a true taste of the Amalfi Coast's maritime heritage.

In the town of Minori, Ristorante Giardiniello is a family-run restaurant with a long tradition of serving delicious, home-cooked meals. The menu features a variety of Italian and Mediterranean dishes, including fresh pasta, seafood, and grilled meats. The restaurant's garden terrace is a lovely spot to enjoy a meal, surrounded by lemon trees and flowering plants. Giardiniello is known for its warm hospitality and commitment to using fresh, local ingredients, making it a favorite among both locals and tourists.

In Maiori, Torre Normanna offers a unique dining experience in a historic Norman tower overlooking the sea. The restaurant's menu features a mix of traditional Italian and contemporary dishes, including seafood risotto, beef fillet with balsamic reduction, and homemade desserts. The stunning views from the tower's terrace, combined with the high-quality cuisine, make Torre Normanna a memorable dining destination. The restaurant also offers a selection of local wines, allowing guests to pair their meal with the perfect glass of wine.

For those looking to explore the culinary traditions of the Amalfi Coast, a visit to the local markets is a must. The markets in towns like Amalfi, Positano, and Maiori offer a wide variety of fresh produce, seafood, and artisanal products. Visitors can sample local cheeses, cured meats, and pastries, as well as purchase ingredients to create their own meals. The vibrant atmosphere and friendly vendors make the markets a delightful place to experience the flavors of the Amalfi Coast.

The Amalfi Coast is home to a diverse array of restaurants and eateries that offer exceptional dining experiences. From Michelin-starred establishments and elegant hotel restaurants to family-run trattorias and beachfront cafes, the region's culinary scene is as varied as it is delicious. Whether you are seeking a romantic dinner with stunning views, a casual meal of fresh seafood, or a taste of traditional Italian cuisine, the Amalfi Coast has something to offer every palate. By exploring the best restaurants and eateries in the region, visitors can enjoy a rich and flavorful journey through the culinary heritage of this beautiful part of Italy.

Street Food and Local Delicacies

The Amalfi Coast is not only renowned for its stunning scenery and historic sites but also for its rich culinary heritage. One of the best ways to experience the region's authentic flavors is through its street food and local delicacies. These offerings provide a direct connection to the area's traditions and culture, allowing visitors to taste the essence of the Amalfi Coast in a casual and accessible way.

One of the most iconic street foods on the Amalfi Coast is the arancini. These are deep-fried rice balls, typically filled with a mixture of ragù (meat sauce), peas, and mozzarella. The rice is cooked with saffron, giving it a distinct golden color. Arancini are crispy on the outside and soft and flavorful on the inside. They are a popular snack and can be found in many local bakeries and street food stalls. Their satisfying combination of textures and flavors makes them a must-try for anyone visiting the region.

Another popular street food is the pizza fritta, or fried pizza. Unlike the traditional baked pizza, pizza fritta is made by frying a dough pocket stuffed with various ingredients such as ricotta, provolone, and salami. The result is a crispy, golden exterior with a warm, gooey filling. This dish is a favorite among locals and visitors alike, providing a unique twist on the classic pizza experience. It is often enjoyed as a quick snack or a light meal.

Sfogliatella is another beloved local delicacy. This pastry, which originated in the nearby city of Naples, is a staple in Amalfi Coast bakeries. Sfogliatella comes in two main varieties: riccia, which has a crispy, layered exterior resembling a seashell, and frolla, which has a smoother, more doughy texture. Both varieties are typically filled with a sweet, creamy mixture of ricotta, semolina, and candied citrus peel. The combination of the crisp pastry and the rich filling makes sfogliatella a delightful treat, perfect for breakfast or an afternoon snack.

Lemon is a central ingredient in many Amalfi Coast delicacies, thanks to the region's abundant lemon groves. One of the most famous lemon-based treats is the delizia al limone, a lemon sponge cake filled with lemon cream and covered with a lemon glaze. This dessert is light, refreshing, and bursting with citrus flavor. It is a perfect representation of the Amalfi Coast's culinary heritage, showcasing the region's love for its locally grown lemons.

Another lemon-based delicacy is the granita al limone, a semi-frozen dessert made from lemon juice, sugar, and water. Granita is similar to sorbet but has a coarser, more crystalline texture. It is incredibly refreshing, especially on a hot summer day. Vendors selling granita can be found throughout the Amalfi Coast, often offering a variety of flavors, but the lemon granita remains the most traditional and popular choice.

Fritto misto is a common sight at street food stalls and local eateries. This dish consists of a mix of deep-fried seafood, such as calamari, shrimp, and small fish. The seafood is lightly battered and fried to perfection, resulting in a crispy and flavorful snack. Fritto misto is typically served with a wedge of lemon and is best enjoyed fresh out of the fryer. It captures the coastal essence of the region, highlighting the bounty of the Mediterranean Sea.

For a more substantial meal, visitors should try the cuoppo, a paper cone filled with a variety of fried goodies. The contents of a cuoppo can vary, but it often includes fritto misto, arancini, zeppole (fried dough balls), and vegetables. This portable and convenient dish is perfect for enjoying while exploring the towns and villages along the coast. Each bite offers a different taste and texture, making it a fun and satisfying way to experience the local cuisine.

In addition to these savory treats, the Amalfi Coast is also known for its sweet delicacies. One such treat is the torta caprese, a rich chocolate and almond cake. This cake is gluten-free, made without any flour, and has a dense, moist texture. It is often dusted with powdered sugar and served with a dollop of whipped cream. The intense chocolate flavor, combined with the nutty taste of almonds, makes torta caprese a favorite dessert among locals and visitors.

Another sweet delight is the babà, a small yeast cake soaked in rum syrup. Originally from Naples, babà has become a popular treat along the Amalfi Coast as well. The cake is light and airy, with a spongy texture that absorbs the sweet, boozy syrup. Babà is often served plain or filled with whipped cream or pastry cream, adding an extra layer of indulgence. This dessert is a testament to the region's rich baking traditions and love for flavorful, satisfying sweets.

No exploration of Amalfi Coast delicacies would be complete without mentioning the region's renowned limoncello. This lemon liqueur is made by steeping lemon peels in alcohol and then mixing the infused alcohol with a simple syrup. The result is a bright, intensely flavored liqueur that is typically served chilled as a digestif. Many local producers sell bottles of limoncello, making it a perfect souvenir to bring home. Sampling limoncello while enjoying the stunning coastal views is an essential part of the Amalfi Coast experience.

The town of Cetara is particularly known for its anchovy products. Cetara is a small fishing village with a long tradition of anchovy fishing and processing. One of the most unique products is colatura di alici, a fish sauce made from anchovy extract. This ancient condiment is used to add a rich, savory flavor to pasta dishes, salads, and vegetables. Visitors can find bottles of colatura di alici in local markets and specialty shops, making it a distinctive and flavorful souvenir.

In addition to these specific dishes and products, the Amalfi Coast is also home to a variety of local markets where visitors can find fresh produce, cheeses, cured meats, and other regional specialties. These markets are a great place to sample local flavors and purchase ingredients to recreate the dishes at home. The vibrant atmosphere and friendly vendors make visiting the markets a delightful and immersive experience.

The street food and local delicacies of the Amalfi Coast offer a rich and diverse culinary experience. From savory treats like arancini and pizza fritta to sweet delights like sfogliatella and delizia al limone, there is something to satisfy every palate. The region's love for fresh, high-quality ingredients and traditional recipes is evident in every bite. Exploring the street food and local delicacies allows visitors to connect with the culture and heritage of the Amalfi Coast in a delicious and memorable way. Whether you are enjoying a simple snack from a street vendor or indulging in a decadent dessert at a local bakery, the flavors of the Amalfi Coast are sure to leave a lasting impression.

Cooking Classes and Food Tours

The Amalfi Coast, known for its breathtaking views and charming towns, is also a paradise for food lovers. The region's culinary traditions are deeply rooted in its history, culture, and geography. One of the most immersive ways to experience this culinary heritage is through cooking classes and food tours. These activities offer visitors the opportunity to learn about local ingredients, traditional recipes, and cooking techniques directly from the experts. Whether you are a novice cook or a seasoned foodie, the Amalfi Coast provides a rich and rewarding culinary journey.

Cooking classes on the Amalfi Coast are an excellent way to delve into the local cuisine. These classes are often held in picturesque settings, such as historic villas, charming farmhouses, or modern cooking schools, providing a beautiful backdrop for your culinary education. One popular destination for cooking classes is the town of Ravello. Here, you can find several cooking schools that offer hands-on classes in a variety of traditional dishes. Participants typically start with a visit to a local market, where they learn to select the freshest ingredients. Back in the kitchen, they are guided by experienced chefs through the preparation of a multi-course meal. Dishes often include homemade pasta, seafood specialties, and classic desserts like tiramisu or lemon cake.

Another renowned cooking school is Mamma Agata's Cooking School in Ravello. Run by the charming and talented Mamma Agata and her family, this school offers a unique and personal cooking experience. Participants are welcomed into Mamma Agata's home and kitchen, where they learn to prepare traditional recipes using fresh, locally sourced ingredients. The class includes a tour of the family's garden, where many of the ingredients are grown. The highlight of the experience is, of course, the meal itself, enjoyed on the terrace with stunning views of the Amalfi Coast.

In Positano, La Cucina del Gusto by Chef Carmen is a popular choice for cooking enthusiasts. Chef Carmen is known for her warm hospitality and expert instruction. Her classes cover a wide range of traditional dishes, from antipasti to desserts. Participants learn to make dishes such as gnocchi, seafood risotto, and panna cotta. The classes are designed to be fun and interactive, with plenty of opportunities to ask questions and get hands-on experience. The atmosphere is relaxed and convivial, making it a great option for couples, families, or solo travelers.

The town of Amalfi also offers several excellent cooking classes. One notable option is the Amalfi Lemon Experience, which combines a cooking class with a tour of a lemon grove. Participants learn about the cultivation and uses of the famous Amalfi lemons, followed by a hands-on cooking class where they prepare lemon-infused dishes such as lemon risotto and lemon tiramisu. The experience is both educational and delicious, providing a deeper appreciation for this iconic ingredient.

Food tours are another fantastic way to explore the culinary delights of the Amalfi Coast. These tours often include visits to local markets, food producers, and restaurants, allowing participants to sample a wide variety of regional specialties. One popular tour is the Taste of Amalfi Food Tour, which takes participants on a guided walk through the historic town of Amalfi. The tour includes stops at a traditional bakery, a family-run limoncello producer, and a local cheese shop. Along the way, participants sample fresh pastries, cheeses, cured meats, and, of course, limoncello. The tour provides a comprehensive overview of the local food culture, with plenty of opportunities to taste and learn.

In the town of Maiori, the Maiori Food and Wine Tour offers a similar experience, with a focus on the region's excellent wines. The tour includes visits to local vineyards and wine cellars, where participants learn about the winemaking process and sample a variety of wines. The tour also includes stops at a local bakery and a traditional trattoria, where participants enjoy a delicious meal paired with local wines. The Maiori Food and Wine Tour is a great way to explore the culinary and viticultural traditions of the Amalfi Coast.

For those interested in a more immersive experience, the Amalfi Coast Cooking Vacation is an excellent option. This multi-day program combines cooking classes, food tours, and cultural excursions, providing a comprehensive introduction to the region's cuisine and culture. Participants stay in a charming villa or hotel and take part in daily cooking classes, where they learn to prepare a variety of traditional dishes. The program also includes visits to local markets, food producers, and historic sites, offering a well-rounded and enriching experience.

One of the highlights of the Amalfi Coast culinary scene is the focus on fresh, locally sourced ingredients. The region's fertile soil and mild climate produce an abundance of high-quality fruits, vegetables, and herbs. Seafood is also a staple of the local diet, with the Mediterranean providing a bounty of fresh fish, shellfish, and other seafood. Many cooking classes and food tours emphasize the importance of using fresh, seasonal ingredients, teaching participants how to select and prepare them for maximum flavor and nutrition.

In addition to the hands-on cooking experiences, many classes and tours also include demonstrations and tastings. Participants might watch a master pasta maker at work, sample a variety of olive oils, or learn about the art of cheese-making. These demonstrations provide valuable insights into the techniques and traditions that define Amalfi Coast cuisine. Tastings are a highlight of any food tour, offering the chance to savor the region's best products and dishes.

Whether it's a freshly baked pastry, a slice of cured meat, or a sip of limoncello, each tasting is an opportunity to experience the flavors of the Amalfi Coast.

Another aspect of the culinary experience on the Amalfi Coast is the emphasis on family and tradition. Many of the cooking classes and food tours are run by families who have been in the business for generations. These families take great pride in sharing their knowledge and traditions with visitors, providing a personal and authentic experience. Participants often feel like they are being welcomed into a local home, rather than just taking a class or tour. This sense of hospitality and community is a key part of the Amalfi Coast's culinary charm.

Cooking classes and food tours on the Amalfi Coast offer a rich and rewarding way to explore the region's culinary heritage. From hands-on cooking classes in picturesque settings to guided food tours that showcase the best local products, these experiences provide a deep and immersive introduction to Amalfi Coast cuisine. Whether you are a novice cook or an experienced foodie, there is something to suit every taste and interest. By participating in these activities, visitors can gain a deeper appreciation for the region's culinary traditions, learn new skills, and enjoy some of the best food and drink the Amalfi Coast has to offer.

Wine Tasting and Vineyards

The Amalfi Coast is a region of Italy known for its breathtaking scenery, historic towns, and rich culinary heritage. One of the most delightful aspects of this culinary heritage is its wine. The combination of the region's unique climate, fertile soil, and centuries-old winemaking traditions results in some truly exceptional wines. Exploring the vineyards and indulging in wine tastings along the Amalfi Coast offers a deep dive into this viticultural paradise.

The Amalfi Coast's winemaking tradition dates back to ancient times, with evidence of viticulture in the region during the Roman era. The unique terroir of the Amalfi Coast, characterized by steep terraced vineyards, volcanic soil, and a Mediterranean climate, creates ideal conditions for growing a variety of grapes. The most common grape varieties in the region include Falanghina, Biancolella, and Ginestra for white wines, and Aglianico and Piedirosso for red wines. These grapes produce wines that are expressive of their environment, offering flavors and aromas that reflect the coastal influence and the minerality of the soil.

One of the best ways to experience the wines of the Amalfi Coast is by visiting the local vineyards. These vineyards are often family-owned and have been passed down through generations, each with its own unique story and approach to winemaking. A visit to a vineyard typically includes a tour of the vineyards and the cellar, followed by a tasting of the estate's wines. This immersive experience provides insight into the winemaking process, from grape cultivation to fermentation and aging, and allows visitors to taste the wines in the place where they are made.

One notable vineyard on the Amalfi Coast is Marisa Cuomo in Furore. This vineyard is known for its dramatic location, with terraced vineyards clinging to the steep cliffs overlooking the sea. Marisa Cuomo produces a range of wines, including the famous Fiorduva, a white wine made from a blend of indigenous grape varieties. The vineyard tour includes a walk through the scenic vineyards, a visit to the ancient cellar carved into the rock, and a tasting of their exquisite wines. The combination of the stunning setting and the exceptional quality of the wines makes Marisa Cuomo a must-visit for wine enthusiasts.

Another excellent vineyard to visit is Tenuta San Francesco in Tramonti. This vineyard is situated in a lush, green valley surrounded by forests and mountains. Tenuta San Francesco specializes in the cultivation of ancient grape varieties, some of which are unique to the region. The vineyard tour includes a walk through the vineyards, where visitors can see the old vines that have been cultivated for generations. The tasting features a selection of their wines, including the award-winning E' Iss red wine, made from Tintore grapes. The warm hospitality and dedication to preserving local traditions make Tenuta San Francesco a highlight of any wine tour on the Amalfi Coast.

In Ravello, Azienda Agricola Montevetrano is a vineyard that has gained international acclaim for its high-quality wines. Montevetrano produces both red and white wines, with their flagship wine being a blend of Aglianico, Cabernet Sauvignon, and Merlot. The vineyard tour includes a walk through the vineyards and a visit to the modern winery, where visitors can learn about the innovative techniques used in their winemaking process. The tasting room offers a stunning view of the vineyards and the surrounding countryside, providing a perfect setting to enjoy their elegant and complex wines.

The town of Maiori is home to the vineyard Reale, which has been producing wine since the early 1900s. Reale is known for its traditional approach to winemaking, using methods that have been passed down through generations. The vineyard tour includes a visit to the old cellar, where the wines are aged in large oak barrels. The tasting features a selection of their wines, including the white Aliseo and the red Borgo di Gete, both of which reflect the unique terroir of the region. The intimate and rustic atmosphere of Reale makes it a charming destination for wine lovers.

In addition to vineyard tours, there are several wine bars and enotecas on the Amalfi Coast where visitors can enjoy wine tastings. These establishments offer a curated selection of local wines, often paired with delicious food. One such place is Enoteca Re Maurì in Vietri sul Mare, which offers an extensive wine list featuring wines from the Amalfi Coast and beyond. The knowledgeable staff can guide visitors through a tasting of different wines, providing insights into the characteristics and history of each one. The cozy and elegant setting of Enoteca Re Maurì makes it an ideal place to relax and savor the flavors of the region.

Another excellent wine bar is Wine & Drugs in Amalfi, known for its eclectic selection of wines and its relaxed, bohemian atmosphere. The wine list includes a variety of local and international wines, with a focus on natural and organic producers. The staff at Wine & Drugs are passionate about wine and are happy to share their knowledge and recommendations with visitors. The bar also offers a selection of small plates and snacks, making it a great spot for a casual and enjoyable wine tasting experience.

For those who prefer a more structured wine tasting experience, several tour operators on the Amalfi Coast offer guided wine tours. These tours typically include visits to multiple vineyards, providing a comprehensive overview of the region's wine culture. One popular option is the Amalfi Coast Wine Tour, which takes participants to several top vineyards and includes tastings, vineyard tours, and a delicious lunch featuring local cuisine. The tour is led by knowledgeable guides who provide insights into the winemaking process and the history of the region's viticulture.

Another recommended tour is the Path of the Gods Wine Tour, which combines a scenic hike along the famous Path of the Gods with visits to local vineyards. The tour includes a guided hike with stunning views of the coastline, followed by visits to vineyards where participants can taste wines and learn about the unique challenges of cultivating grapes in this dramatic landscape. The combination of outdoor adventure and wine tasting makes this tour a memorable and enriching experience.

The Amalfi Coast is also home to several wine festivals and events that celebrate the region's viticultural heritage. One notable event is the Festa del Vino in Tramonti, which takes place in August. The festival features wine tastings, food stalls, live music, and cultural performances, providing a festive and convivial atmosphere. Visitors can sample a variety of wines from local producers and enjoy the vibrant ambiance of this charming village.

The Amalfi Coast offers a wealth of opportunities for wine enthusiasts to explore and enjoy the region's exceptional wines. From visiting historic vineyards and participating in wine tastings to exploring local wine bars and joining guided wine tours, there are countless ways to experience the rich viticultural heritage of the region. The unique terroir, combined with the dedication and passion of local winemakers, results in wines that are expressive, flavorful, and deeply connected to the land. Whether you are a casual wine drinker or a serious oenophile, the Amalfi Coast provides a diverse and rewarding wine journey that is sure to leave a lasting impression.

CHAPTER 8

ACTIVITIES AND ADVENTURES

Outdoor Activities: Hiking, Biking, and Watersports

The Amalfi Coast, renowned for its stunning landscapes and historic towns, is also a paradise for outdoor enthusiasts. The region offers a variety of activities that allow visitors to fully appreciate its natural beauty and diverse terrain. From hiking and biking to watersports, there are countless ways to explore and enjoy the Amalfi Coast's magnificent scenery.

One of the most popular outdoor activities on the Amalfi Coast is hiking. The region boasts a network of trails that offer breathtaking views and access to some of the most picturesque spots. One of the most famous trails is the Path of the Gods, or Sentiero degli Dei. This trail runs from the village of Bomerano in Agerola to Nocelle, a hamlet above Positano. The Path of the Gods offers spectacular panoramic views of the coastline, the sea, and the surrounding mountains. The trail is well-marked and suitable for hikers of all levels, making it a must-do for nature lovers and adventure seekers. Along the way, hikers pass through terraced vineyards, ancient ruins, and charming villages, providing a glimpse into the rich history and culture of the region.

Another fantastic hiking trail is the Valle delle Ferriere, a lush nature reserve located near Amalfi. This trail takes hikers through a verdant valley filled with waterfalls, rare plants, and ancient ruins. The trail follows the course of the Canneto River, passing through dense forests and alongside cascading streams. The Valle delle Ferriere is a haven for nature lovers, offering a tranquil escape from the bustling coastal towns. The trail also leads to the remains of old ironworks, providing insight into the region's industrial past.

For a more challenging hike, the trail to Monte Tre Calli offers spectacular panoramic views of the Amalfi Coast and the Bay of Naples. This trail starts in the village of Bomerano and ascends to the summit of Monte Tre Calli, providing a strenuous but rewarding hike. The trail passes through rugged terrain, pine forests, and rocky outcrops, culminating in breathtaking views from the summit. On clear days, hikers can see as far as the island of Capri and the distant mountains of Calabria.

In addition to these well-known trails, the Amalfi Coast offers numerous other hiking opportunities that cater to different interests and abilities. The Sentiero dei Limoni, or Path of the Lemons, takes hikers through the terraced lemon groves that are characteristic of the region. This trail runs between the towns of Maiori and Minori, offering stunning views of the coastline and the lush lemon orchards. The scent of lemon blossoms fills the air as hikers traverse the path, providing a sensory experience that is uniquely Amalfi. The trail is relatively easy and suitable for all ages, making it a great option for families and casual hikers.

Biking is another popular outdoor activity on the Amalfi Coast. The region's winding coastal roads and scenic routes provide an exhilarating experience for cyclists. One of the most scenic routes is the ride along the Amalfi Drive, or SS163, which runs from Sorrento to Salerno. This road hugs the coastline, offering stunning views of the sea and the cliffs. The ride is challenging, with its narrow lanes and steep inclines, but the breathtaking scenery makes it well worth the effort. Cyclists can stop in the various towns along the route, such as Positano, Amalfi, and Ravello, to explore and rest before continuing their journey.

For those looking for a more relaxed biking experience, the roads around the town of Agerola offer beautiful scenery and less traffic. Agerola is located in the hills above the Amalfi Coast and is known for its pastoral landscapes and charming villages. The roads here are quieter and less crowded, making it an ideal location for leisurely rides. Cyclists can enjoy the fresh mountain air and the stunning views of the coast from above, providing a different perspective of the region.

Mountain biking is also an option for those seeking a more adventurous experience. The rugged terrain and diverse landscapes of the Amalfi Coast provide excellent opportunities for off-road cycling. There are several trails and paths that cater to mountain bikers, ranging from easy to challenging. These trails take cyclists through forests, over hills, and along rocky ridges, offering a thrilling and immersive experience. One popular mountain biking route is the Sentiero degli Dei, which can be traversed by experienced cyclists who are looking for a challenging and rewarding ride.

Watersports are another major attraction on the Amalfi Coast, with its clear blue waters and stunning coastal scenery providing the perfect backdrop for aquatic adventures. One of the most popular watersports is kayaking. Kayaking allows visitors to explore the coastline at their own pace, discovering hidden coves, sea caves, and secluded beaches. There are several companies that offer kayak rentals and guided tours, providing all the necessary equipment and instruction. One popular kayaking route is from Amalfi to the Grotta dello Smeraldo, a stunning sea cave known for its emerald-green waters. The cave can be explored by kayak, offering a unique and memorable experience.

Stand-up paddleboarding (SUP) is another popular watersport on the Amalfi Coast. This activity combines elements of surfing and kayaking, allowing participants to paddle along the coastline while standing on a board. SUP is a great way to enjoy the scenery and get a full-body workout at the same time. The calm waters of the Amalfi Coast are ideal for paddleboarding, providing a serene and beautiful environment for this activity. There are several rental shops and tour operators that offer SUP equipment and guided tours, catering to both beginners and experienced paddleboarders.

Snorkeling and scuba diving are also popular activities on the Amalfi Coast, with its clear waters and diverse marine life providing excellent opportunities for underwater exploration. There are several dive centers and tour operators that offer snorkeling and diving excursions, providing all the necessary equipment and instruction. The waters around the Amalfi Coast are home to a variety of marine species, including colorful fish, octopuses, and sea urchins. Some popular dive sites include the underwater caves and reefs near Praiano and the submerged Roman ruins near Baia.

For those who prefer to stay on the water's surface, boat tours and sailing trips offer a relaxing and scenic way to explore the Amalfi Coast. There are several companies that offer boat rentals, guided tours, and sailing excursions, providing a variety of options to suit different interests and budgets. Boat tours often include stops at popular attractions such as the Grotta dello Smeraldo, the island of Capri, and the town of Positano. Sailing trips provide a more leisurely and intimate experience, allowing participants to enjoy the beauty of the coastline while cruising along the azure waters.

In addition to these specific activities, the Amalfi Coast offers numerous other opportunities for outdoor adventure and exploration. The region's diverse landscapes and natural beauty provide a perfect setting for activities such as rock climbing, canyoning, and paragliding. Rock climbing enthusiasts can find several climbing spots along the coast, with routes that cater to different skill levels. Canyoning involves descending through narrow gorges and waterfalls, providing an exhilarating and immersive experience. Paragliding offers a bird's-eye view of the stunning coastline, allowing participants to soar above the cliffs and enjoy the breathtaking scenery from above.

The Amalfi Coast is a paradise for outdoor enthusiasts, offering a wide range of activities that allow visitors to fully appreciate its natural beauty and diverse terrain. From hiking and biking to watersports and beyond, there are countless ways to explore and enjoy the magnificent scenery of this stunning region. Whether you are seeking a leisurely stroll through lemon groves, an exhilarating mountain bike ride, or an underwater adventure, the Amalfi Coast provides a rich and rewarding outdoor experience that is sure to leave a lasting impression.

Boat Tours and Cruises

The Amalfi Coast, renowned for its stunning cliffs, crystal-clear waters, and charming coastal towns, offers a unique and unforgettable experience through boat tours and cruises. These maritime adventures provide a distinctive perspective on the region's natural beauty and historical landmarks.

Exploring the Amalfi Coast by boat allows visitors to access hidden coves, pristine beaches, and picturesque villages that are often difficult to reach by land.

One of the most popular ways to experience the Amalfi Coast by sea is through guided boat tours. These tours typically last a few hours to a full day and provide an in-depth exploration of the coastline. A typical boat tour includes visits to several iconic spots such as Positano, Amalfi, and Ravello, as well as hidden gems like secluded beaches and sea caves. The tours are often led by knowledgeable local guides who share insights into the region's history, culture, and natural features.

A highly recommended tour is the Amalfi Coast Full-Day Boat Tour. This tour departs from various towns such as Sorrento, Positano, or Amalfi and includes stops at key locations along the coast. Participants can expect to visit the charming town of Positano, known for its colorful buildings and narrow, winding streets. The tour also typically includes a stop at the Grotta dello Smeraldo, or Emerald Grotto, a sea cave famous for its emerald-green waters. The final destination is often the historic town of Amalfi, where visitors can explore its impressive cathedral and enjoy a leisurely lunch at a seaside restaurant.

For a more personalized experience, private boat tours are an excellent option. These tours offer the flexibility to customize the itinerary according to the preferences of the participants. Private tours often include exclusive access to lesser-known spots and the opportunity to spend more time at preferred locations. One popular private tour is the Capri and Amalfi Coast Private Boat Tour, which combines visits to the beautiful island of Capri with an exploration of the Amalfi Coast. This tour allows participants to swim in the Blue Grotto, relax on the beach, and enjoy a personalized commentary from the captain.

Sunset cruises are another popular choice for visitors looking to experience the Amalfi Coast's magical evening ambiance. These cruises typically depart in the late afternoon and sail along the coast as the sun sets over the Mediterranean Sea. The breathtaking colors of the sunset reflecting off the water create a truly memorable experience. Many sunset cruises also include a glass of Prosecco or a light aperitivo, adding a touch of elegance to the journey. The Positano Sunset Cruise is particularly popular, offering stunning views of the coastline and the opportunity to see the town of Positano illuminated at night.

For those interested in a more leisurely and luxurious experience, multi-day cruises along the Amalfi Coast and surrounding areas are available. These cruises provide the ultimate in comfort and relaxation, with onboard accommodations and amenities. One notable option is the Amalfi Coast and Aeolian Islands Cruise, which spans several days and includes visits to the beautiful Aeolian Islands, such as Lipari, Stromboli, and Vulcano, in addition to the Amalfi Coast. These cruises offer the chance to explore a wider area while enjoying the luxury of a fully equipped yacht or small cruise ship.

In addition to these guided tours and cruises, the Amalfi Coast also offers opportunities for more independent exploration. Boat rentals are widely available, allowing visitors to captain their own vessels and discover the coast at their own pace. Rentals range from small motorboats and dinghies to larger yachts and sailboats. Renting a boat provides the freedom to explore hidden coves, stop for a swim in secluded bays, and visit coastal villages on your own schedule. Many rental companies also offer the option to hire a skipper, providing local expertise and navigation skills while you relax and enjoy the journey.

Sailing enthusiasts will find the Amalfi Coast an ideal destination for their passion. The region's favorable winds and stunning scenery make it a popular choice for sailing tours and charters. Sailing tours often include stops at key attractions and offer the chance to learn about sailing techniques from experienced skippers. One popular option is the Amalfi Coast Sailing Tour, which includes visits to Positano, Capri, and the lesser-known town of Cetara, known for its fishing heritage and delicious anchovies. Participants can enjoy the thrill of sailing while taking in the beautiful coastline.

For a unique and adventurous experience, snorkeling and diving tours are available along the Amalfi Coast. The region's clear waters and diverse marine life provide excellent conditions for underwater exploration. Snorkeling tours typically visit spots with abundant marine life, such as the Marine Protected Area of Punta Campanella. These tours often include equipment rental and guided instruction, making them accessible to beginners and experienced snorkelers alike. Diving tours offer the chance to explore underwater caves, shipwrecks, and vibrant coral reefs. The Gaiola Underwater Park, located near Naples, is a popular diving destination known for its archaeological ruins and rich marine biodiversity.

Fishing enthusiasts will also find plenty of opportunities to indulge their hobby on the Amalfi Coast. Fishing tours and charters are available, offering the chance to catch a variety of fish species, such as sea bass, tuna, and mackerel. These tours often include all necessary equipment and the expertise of a local fisherman who knows the best spots and techniques for a successful fishing trip. The experience of fishing in the Mediterranean waters, surrounded by the stunning scenery of the Amalfi Coast, is both relaxing and rewarding.

Another unique way to explore the Amalfi Coast by boat is through culinary tours that combine sightseeing with gourmet experiences. These tours often include stops at coastal towns and fishing villages, where participants can sample local delicacies and enjoy meals at seaside restaurants. One popular option is the Amalfi Coast Food and Wine Cruise, which includes visits to local vineyards and olive groves, tastings of regional wines and olive oils, and a traditional Italian cooking class on board. These culinary tours provide a delicious and immersive way to experience the culture and flavors of the Amalfi Coast.

Boat tours and cruises on the Amalfi Coast offer a wide range of experiences that allow visitors to fully appreciate the region's natural beauty and cultural heritage. From guided tours and private charters to sunset cruises and multi-day adventures, there are countless ways to explore the coastline by sea. Whether you are seeking relaxation, adventure, or a combination of both, the Amalfi Coast provides a rich and rewarding maritime experience that is sure to leave a lasting impression. With its stunning landscapes, clear blue waters, and charming coastal towns, exploring the Amalfi Coast by boat is an unforgettable journey that captures the essence of this magical region.

Guided Tours and Day Trips

The Amalfi Coast, with its dramatic cliffs, vibrant towns, and stunning sea views, is a destination that offers countless opportunities for exploration and discovery. Guided tours and day trips are excellent ways to experience the richness of this region, providing structured and informative experiences that highlight the best of what the Amalfi Coast has to offer. From historical sites and natural wonders to culinary delights and artisanal crafts, these tours cater to a variety of interests and preferences.

One of the most popular types of guided tours on the Amalfi Coast is the historical and cultural tour. These tours typically include visits to significant landmarks and sites that offer insight into the region's rich history and heritage. A highly recommended historical tour is the Pompeii and Amalfi Coast Day Trip. This tour usually begins with a visit to the ancient ruins of Pompeii, a UNESCO World Heritage site. Participants can explore the well-preserved remains of this Roman city, buried by the eruption of Mount Vesuvius in 79 AD. Guided by an expert, visitors learn about the daily life of Pompeii's inhabitants and the catastrophic event that led to its preservation. Following the visit to Pompeii, the tour continues along the Amalfi Coast, with stops in picturesque towns such as Positano and Amalfi. These stops provide a perfect blend of history, culture, and breathtaking scenery.

Another excellent historical tour is the Ravello and Villa Cimbrone Day Trip. This tour focuses on the beautiful hilltop town of Ravello, known for its historic villas and stunning gardens. Participants visit Villa Rufolo, a medieval villa with exquisite gardens and panoramic views of the coastline. The tour also includes a visit to Villa Cimbrone, renowned for its Terrace of Infinity, which offers one of the most breathtaking views in Italy. The tour provides detailed information about the history of Ravello and the significance of these villas, making it a must-do for history and architecture enthusiasts.

For those interested in the natural beauty of the Amalfi Coast, guided nature tours are an excellent option. The Path of the Gods Hiking Tour is one of the most popular nature tours, offering a chance to experience the region's stunning landscapes up close. This guided hike takes participants along the Sentiero degli Dei, or Path of the Gods, a trail that runs from Bomerano to Nocelle. The hike offers spectacular views of the coastline, the sea, and the surrounding mountains. Along the way, the guide provides insights into the flora and fauna of the region, as well as the history and legends associated with the trail. The Path of the Gods Hiking Tour is suitable for hikers of all levels and provides a rewarding and immersive experience in nature.

Another recommended nature tour is the Valle delle Ferriere Walking Tour. This tour explores the lush Valle delle Ferriere nature reserve, located near Amalfi. Participants walk through a verdant valley filled with waterfalls, rare plants, and ancient ruins. The tour includes a visit to the remains of old ironworks, providing a glimpse into the region's industrial past. The guide shares information about the unique ecosystem of the valley and the various plant and animal species that inhabit it. The Valle delle Ferriere Walking Tour is a peaceful and educational experience, perfect for nature lovers and those seeking a tranquil escape from the bustling towns.

Food and wine tours are also a highlight of the Amalfi Coast, offering a chance to savor the region's culinary delights and learn about its gastronomic traditions. The Amalfi Coast Food and Wine Tour is a popular choice, combining visits to local vineyards, olive groves, and food producers with tastings of regional specialties. Participants sample local wines, olive oils, cheeses, and cured meats, gaining a deeper understanding of the region's culinary heritage. The tour often includes a visit to a traditional limoncello producer, where participants learn about the production process and taste this iconic lemon liqueur. The Amalfi Coast Food and Wine Tour is a delicious and informative experience, perfect for foodies and wine enthusiasts.

Another excellent culinary tour is the Cooking Class and Market Tour. This tour typically begins with a visit to a local market, where participants learn about the fresh, seasonal ingredients used in traditional Amalfi Coast cuisine. The tour guide, often a local chef, provides tips on selecting the best produce and explains the role of these ingredients in the region's culinary traditions. Following the market visit, participants take part in a hands-on cooking class, where they learn to prepare a multi-course meal using the ingredients they have selected. The class usually concludes with a shared meal, allowing participants to enjoy the fruits of their labor while taking in the beautiful surroundings. The Cooking Class and Market Tour offers a fun and interactive way to experience the flavors of the Amalfi Coast.

For those interested in exploring the artistic side of the Amalfi Coast, art and craft tours provide a unique and engaging experience. The Vietri sul Mare Ceramics Tour is a must-do for anyone interested in the region's famous ceramics. This tour includes visits to several ceramics workshops and boutiques in Vietri sul Mare, where participants can see artisans at work and learn about the techniques and traditions of this craft. The tour often includes a visit to the Ceramics Museum, which showcases a collection of historic and contemporary ceramic pieces. Participants have the opportunity to purchase unique, handmade ceramics as souvenirs, making this tour both educational and practical.

The Amalfi Coast Photography Tour is another excellent option for those interested in capturing the beauty of the region through the lens. Led by a professional photographer, this tour takes participants to some of the most picturesque spots along the coast, providing tips and techniques for taking stunning photographs. The tour includes visits to iconic locations such as Positano, Amalfi, and Ravello, as well as lesser-known viewpoints and hidden gems. The guide offers insights into composition, lighting, and camera settings, helping participants improve their photography skills while creating lasting memories of their trip.

For visitors looking to explore beyond the Amalfi Coast, day trips to nearby destinations offer a variety of exciting possibilities. One popular day trip is the Capri Island Tour, which includes a boat ride to the beautiful island of Capri. Participants can explore the island's charming towns, visit the famous Blue Grotto, and take a chairlift to the top of Mount Solaro for panoramic views. The tour often includes free time to shop, dine, and relax on the island, providing a perfect combination of guided activities and independent exploration.

Another recommended day trip is the Paestum and Mozzarella Farm Tour. This tour takes participants to the ancient Greek ruins of Paestum, home to some of the best-preserved Greek temples in the world. The guide provides detailed information about the history and significance of these temples, offering a fascinating glimpse into the ancient past. Following the visit to Paestum, the tour continues to a local mozzarella farm, where participants can see the production process of this delicious cheese and enjoy a tasting. The Paestum and Mozzarella Farm Tour combines history, culture, and culinary delights, making it a well-rounded and enjoyable experience.

The Naples and Pompeii Day Trip is another popular option, offering a chance to explore the vibrant city of Naples and the ancient ruins of Pompeii in one day. The tour typically includes a guided walk through the historic center of Naples, with visits to landmarks such as the Royal Palace, the San Carlo Opera House, and the Naples Cathedral. The tour continues with a visit to Pompeii, where participants can explore the well-preserved ruins and learn about the daily life of the ancient Romans. The Naples and Pompeii Day Trip provides a comprehensive introduction to the history and culture of this fascinating region.

Guided tours and day trips on the Amalfi Coast offer a wide range of experiences that cater to different interests and preferences. From historical and cultural tours to nature hikes, food and wine tastings, art and craft workshops, and day trips to nearby destinations, there are countless ways to explore and enjoy the beauty and richness of the Amalfi Coast. These tours provide a structured and informative experience, ensuring that visitors can fully appreciate the unique charm and heritage of this stunning region. Whether you are a history buff, a nature lover, a foodie, or an art enthusiast, the Amalfi Coast offers a diverse and rewarding array of guided tours and day trips that are sure to leave a lasting impression.

Wellness and Spa Experiences

The Amalfi Coast is synonymous with breathtaking views, rich history, and luxurious experiences. Among its many attractions, the region is also a premier destination for wellness and spa experiences. Whether you are looking to unwind with a soothing massage, rejuvenate with a facial, or immerse yourself in holistic treatments, the Amalfi Coast offers a range of top-tier wellness options. These experiences are designed to cater to those seeking relaxation and rejuvenation amidst the stunning backdrop of this

Mediterranean paradise. This detailed guide will provide a comprehensive and informative overview of the best wellness and spa experiences available along the Amalfi Coast, ensuring that visitors can make the most of their time in this enchanting region.

One of the most renowned wellness destinations on the Amalfi Coast is the Monastero Santa Rosa Hotel & Spa. Perched on a cliff above the sea, this former monastery has been transformed into a luxurious hotel and spa, offering a serene and exclusive retreat. The spa at Monastero Santa Rosa is known for its holistic approach to wellness, combining modern techniques with ancient healing traditions. The facility features a thermal suite with a tepidarium, steam room, sauna, and hydrotherapy pool, all designed to detoxify and rejuvenate the body. Guests can choose from a variety of treatments, including massages, facials, and body scrubs, each tailored to individual needs and preferences. The spa also offers bespoke wellness programs, such as yoga and meditation sessions, aimed at promoting physical and mental well-being. The stunning views of the coastline and the tranquil atmosphere make the Monastero Santa Rosa Spa a haven for relaxation and healing.

Another exceptional wellness destination is the Caruso, A Belmond Hotel, in Ravello. This historic hotel, set in a beautifully restored 11th-century building, boasts a world-class spa that offers a range of luxurious treatments. The spa features indoor and outdoor treatment rooms, allowing guests to enjoy their therapies while taking in the breathtaking views of the Amalfi Coast. Signature treatments include the Caruso Lemon Massage, which uses locally sourced lemon oil to invigorate and refresh the body, and the Mediterranean Ritual, a full-body treatment that combines exfoliation, massage, and a nourishing body wrap. The spa also offers a variety of beauty treatments, such as facials, manicures, and pedicures, ensuring that guests leave feeling pampered and rejuvenated. The Caruso's infinity pool, overlooking the coastline, provides an additional opportunity for relaxation and contemplation.

In Positano, the Le Sirenuse Hotel offers an exquisite spa experience that blends traditional techniques with contemporary luxury. The Sirenuse Spa features a range of treatments inspired by the surrounding landscape and local ingredients. Guests can indulge in the Positano Delight, a signature treatment that includes a citrus body scrub, a relaxing massage, and a hydrating facial. The spa also offers bespoke wellness programs, including yoga and Pilates classes, aimed at enhancing physical fitness and mental clarity. The serene atmosphere, coupled with the attentive service and stunning views, makes the Sirenuse Spa a standout destination for wellness enthusiasts.

The Amalfi Coast is also home to several boutique wellness retreats that offer personalized and intimate experiences. One such retreat is the Casa Angelina in Praiano. This chic and contemporary hotel features a wellness center that focuses on holistic health and well-being. The spa offers a range of treatments, from classic massages and facials to innovative therapies such as chromotherapy and aromatherapy. The wellness center also includes a fitness room, an outdoor pool, and a sauna, providing guests with multiple options for relaxation and exercise. Casa Angelina's tranquil setting, combined with its modern amenities and personalized service, creates an ideal environment for rejuvenation and relaxation.

For those seeking a more immersive wellness experience, the Amalfi Coast offers several specialized retreats and programs. The Yoga and Wellness Retreat at the Il San Pietro di Positano is a popular choice for those looking to deepen their yoga practice and enhance their overall well-being. This retreat includes daily yoga and meditation sessions, led by experienced instructors, as well as workshops on topics such as nutrition, mindfulness, and holistic health. Participants also have the opportunity to enjoy the hotel's spa facilities, which include a Turkish bath, a hydrotherapy pool, and a range of therapeutic treatments. The combination of yoga, wellness education, and luxurious amenities makes this retreat a transformative and enriching experience.

The Amalfi Coast's natural beauty also provides ample opportunities for outdoor wellness activities. Many wellness programs incorporate outdoor elements, such as hiking, swimming, and nature walks, to enhance the overall experience. The Path of the Gods, a famous hiking trail that runs from Bomerano to Nocelle, is a popular choice for wellness enthusiasts. This trail offers stunning views of the coastline and the sea, providing a serene and invigorating environment for physical activity and contemplation. Guided hikes, often combined with yoga sessions and mindfulness practices, allow participants to connect with nature and experience the therapeutic benefits of the outdoors.

Another unique wellness experience on the Amalfi Coast is the Limoncello Therapy at the Hotel Santa Caterina in Amalfi. This innovative treatment uses the region's famous lemons to create a range of therapeutic products, including body scrubs, massages, and facials. The natural oils and extracts from the lemons are known for their detoxifying and rejuvenating properties, making them an ideal ingredient for wellness treatments. The Limoncello Therapy also includes a visit to the hotel's lemon grove, where guests can learn about the cultivation and uses of this iconic fruit. This unique experience combines the benefits of nature with the luxury of a world-class spa, creating a memorable and refreshing wellness experience.

For those interested in combining wellness with culinary delights, the Amalfi Coast offers several food and wellness retreats that focus on healthy and delicious cuisine. The Mediterranean Wellness Retreat at the Palazzo Avino in

Ravello is a standout option. This retreat includes cooking classes with a focus on healthy Mediterranean cuisine, as well as wellness workshops and spa treatments. Participants learn to prepare nutritious and flavorful dishes using fresh, local ingredients, while also enjoying the hotel's luxurious spa facilities. The combination of culinary education and wellness treatments provides a holistic approach to health and well-being, making this retreat a unique and enriching experience.

The Amalfi Coast's commitment to wellness is also evident in its numerous wellness festivals and events. The Ravello Wellness Festival, held annually in the beautiful town of Ravello, is a celebration of health and well-being. The festival features a range of activities, including yoga and meditation sessions, wellness workshops, and fitness classes. Participants can also enjoy wellness treatments, healthy food, and live music, creating a vibrant and uplifting atmosphere. The festival's focus on holistic health and community well-being makes it a highlight of the wellness calendar on the Amalfi Coast.

The Amalfi Coast offers a diverse and rich array of wellness and spa experiences that cater to different needs and preferences. From luxurious hotel spas and boutique wellness retreats to outdoor activities and specialized programs, there are countless ways to relax, rejuvenate, and enhance your well-being in this stunning region. Whether you are seeking a tranquil retreat, a transformative wellness program, or a unique therapeutic experience, the Amalfi Coast provides the perfect setting for a journey of health and relaxation. The combination of natural beauty, luxurious amenities, and personalized service ensures that visitors leave feeling refreshed, revitalized, and inspired.

Shopping in Amalfi Coast

The Amalfi Coast is not only a place of stunning natural beauty and rich history, but it also offers a vibrant shopping experience that reflects the unique culture and traditions of the region. Visitors to the Amalfi Coast will find a diverse range of shopping options, from high-end boutiques and artisan workshops to bustling local markets. Shopping here is not just about purchasing souvenirs; it's an opportunity to immerse oneself in the local way of life and discover the craftsmanship and creativity that define this enchanting part of Italy.

One of the most iconic and sought-after items on the Amalfi Coast is the locally produced ceramics. The town of Vietri sul Mare is particularly famous for its vibrant and colorful ceramics, known as "ceramica vietrese." These ceramics are characterized by their bright colors and intricate designs, often featuring local motifs such as lemons, fish, and coastal landscapes. The tradition of ceramics in Vietri sul Mare dates back to the 15th century, and today, the town is home to numerous workshops and boutiques where skilled artisans continue to create beautiful pieces. Visitors can find a wide range of items, from decorative plates and vases to tiles and kitchenware. Each piece is often hand-painted, making it a unique work of art. Some of the most renowned shops include Ceramica Artistica Solimene and Ceramica Pinto, both of which offer an extensive selection of handcrafted ceramics.

Another important craft in the region is paper-making, which has been practiced in Amalfi since the 12th century. Amalfi paper, or "carta di Amalfi," is renowned for its high quality and distinctive texture. Made from cotton and linen fibers, this handmade paper is often used for writing, printing, and bookbinding. Visitors can learn about the traditional paper-making process at the Paper Museum (Museo della Carta) in Amalfi, which is housed in a historic paper mill. The museum offers guided tours and demonstrations, providing insight into the techniques and history of this ancient craft. In addition to the museum, there are several shops in Amalfi where visitors can purchase beautiful stationery, journals, and other paper products made from Amalfi paper. These items make for elegant and unique souvenirs that capture the essence of the region's artisanal heritage.

Textiles are another significant craft on the Amalfi Coast, with a particular emphasis on hand-loomed fabrics and intricate embroidery. In the town of Positano, visitors can find shops that specialize in linen clothing and accessories, reflecting the town's long tradition of textile production. These shops offer a variety of handmade items, including dresses, shirts, scarves, and bags, all crafted from high-quality natural fibers. The vibrant colors and unique designs make these textiles a perfect souvenir or gift. One notable shop is Emporio Le Sirenuse, which offers a range of luxury clothing and home goods inspired by the Amalfi Coast's heritage and aesthetics.

Food products are also a highlight of the shopping experience on the Amalfi Coast. The region is famous for its lemons, which are used to make a variety of delicious products, including limoncello, a popular lemon liqueur. Visitors can find limoncello in many shops and markets, often packaged in beautifully decorated bottles. Some shops, such as Limonoro in Amalfi, offer tastings and tours, allowing visitors to learn about the production process and sample different varieties of limoncello. In addition to limoncello, the Amalfi Coast is known for its lemon-infused olive oil, honey, and pastries, all of which make excellent gifts and souvenirs.

The town of Minori is famous for its pasta, particularly a type known as "ndunderi," which dates back to Roman times. Local shops and markets offer a variety of handmade pasta, as well as other traditional food products such as anchovy sauce (colatura di alici) from Cetara, and fig jam from the hills above Amalfi. These artisanal food products provide a taste of the region's culinary heritage and are a delight for food lovers. Visitors can also find a selection of local wines, olive oils, and balsamic vinegars, which are produced in the surrounding countryside and make for delicious and memorable souvenirs.

Leather goods are another specialty of the Amalfi Coast, with artisans creating high-quality items such as sandals, bags, and belts. In Positano, visitors can find shops that specialize in handmade leather sandals, a tradition that dates back to the 1960s. These sandals are often customized to fit the customer's feet and can be embellished with a variety of decorative elements. Some of the most well-known shops include Safari Sandals and Nana Positano, both of which offer a range of beautifully crafted leather goods. These items are not only stylish and durable but also reflect the region's artisanal expertise.

Jewelry is another popular souvenir from the Amalfi Coast, with many shops offering handcrafted pieces that incorporate local materials and traditional designs. Coral and cameos are particularly prominent, with artisans creating intricate necklaces, bracelets, and earrings that capture the beauty of the sea and the history of the region. Visitors can find a variety of jewelry shops in towns like Amalfi and Positano, where skilled craftsmen continue to produce exquisite pieces that make for timeless and meaningful souvenirs.

In addition to individual artisan shops, the markets on the Amalfi Coast offer a vibrant and lively atmosphere where visitors can shop for a wide range of local crafts and souvenirs. The markets are held on specific days in different towns, each offering a unique selection of goods. The market in Amalfi, held on Wednesdays, is one of the largest and most diverse, featuring stalls selling everything from fresh fruit and vegetables to clothing and ceramics. The market in Maiori, held on Fridays, is another popular destination, offering a wide range of local products and crafts. These markets provide an excellent opportunity to explore the region's artisanal offerings and find unique and high-quality souvenirs.

The artisans on the Amalfi Coast are known for their skill and creativity, and many of them are happy to share their knowledge and techniques with visitors. Some workshops and studios offer classes and demonstrations, allowing visitors to learn about the traditional crafts and even try their hand at making their own pieces. These experiences provide a deeper connection to the local culture and a greater appreciation for the craftsmanship that goes into creating these beautiful items. Whether you are interested in ceramics, textiles, paper-making, or any other craft, there are opportunities to engage with the artisans and gain insight into their work.

Fashion is another key element of the shopping experience on the Amalfi Coast. The region is home to several boutiques and designer shops that offer a range of stylish clothing and accessories. Positano, in particular, is known for its fashion boutiques, which offer a mix of high-end designer labels and locally made garments. Visitors can find everything from elegant evening wear to casual beachwear, all reflecting the chic and sophisticated style of the Amalfi Coast. One notable boutique is La Bottega di Brunella, which specializes in handmade linen clothing that embodies the relaxed and effortless elegance of the region.

For those interested in home decor and furnishings, the Amalfi Coast offers a range of shops that specialize in artisanal and antique pieces. Visitors can find everything from hand-painted ceramics and intricate lacework to vintage furniture and decorative items. These shops often feature unique and one-of-a-kind pieces that add a touch of Mediterranean charm to any home. One such shop is Il Laboratorio, located in Amalfi, which offers a selection of handcrafted ceramics, textiles, and home accessories that reflect the region's rich artistic heritage.

Perfumes and cosmetics are also popular souvenirs from the Amalfi Coast, with several shops offering a range of products made from local ingredients. The town of Ravello, in particular, is known for its perfumeries, which create fragrances inspired by the scents of the region. Visitors can find perfumes made from Amalfi lemons, Mediterranean herbs, and other local botanicals, providing a sensory reminder of their visit. One notable perfumery is Profumi di Positano, which offers a range of fragrances and skincare products made from natural ingredients sourced from the Amalfi Coast.

Shopping on the Amalfi Coast offers a rich and diverse array of experiences that reflect the region's cultural heritage and artistic traditions. From vibrant ceramics and handmade paper to luxurious textiles and delicious food products, there is something for everyone to discover and enjoy. By exploring the artisan shops, markets, and boutiques, visitors can gain a deeper understanding of the local culture, support the artisans who keep these traditions alive, and take home unique and meaningful souvenirs from their time on the Amalfi Coast. Whether you are looking for a special gift, a taste of the local cuisine, or a beautifully crafted piece of art, the shopping experiences of the Amalfi Coast provide a wealth of opportunities to experience the region's rich cultural heritage.

CHAPTER 9

TRAVELING SOLO

Safety Tips for Solo Travelers

The Amalfi Coast is one of the most beautiful and captivating destinations in Italy, known for its stunning landscapes, charming towns, and rich cultural heritage. It is a popular destination for solo travelers who are drawn to its picturesque scenery, delicious cuisine, and vibrant local culture. Traveling solo can be a liberating and enriching experience, but it also comes with its own set of challenges and considerations. To ensure a safe and enjoyable trip to the Amalfi Coast, solo travelers should be well-prepared and mindful of certain safety tips.

First and foremost, it is important for solo travelers to conduct thorough research and planning before embarking on their journey. Understanding the local culture, customs, and laws can help travelers navigate their surroundings more confidently and respectfully. Familiarizing oneself with the layout of the towns, the locations of key attractions, and the available transportation options can also help solo travelers feel more at ease and prepared. It is advisable to have a general itinerary in place, including planned activities, accommodation details, and transportation schedules. Having a well-thought-out plan can reduce stress and provide a sense of security while traveling alone.

Choosing the right accommodation is a crucial aspect of ensuring safety as a solo traveler. The Amalfi Coast offers a wide range of accommodation options, from luxurious hotels and charming bed and breakfasts to budget-friendly hostels and vacation rentals. Solo travelers should prioritize accommodations that are well-reviewed, centrally located, and offer secure facilities. Staying in a reputable hotel or guesthouse can provide an added layer of safety, as these establishments often have security measures in place and staff available to assist with any concerns. Additionally, choosing accommodation in well-populated and well-lit areas can enhance safety, especially when returning at night.

While exploring the Amalfi Coast, solo travelers should be mindful of their surroundings and exercise caution, particularly in crowded or unfamiliar areas. Pickpocketing and petty theft can occur in tourist-heavy locations, so it is important to keep valuables secure and out of sight. Using a money belt or a hidden pouch to carry important documents, cash, and credit cards can help protect against theft. It is also advisable to avoid displaying expensive jewelry or electronic devices, as this can attract unwanted attention. When using public transportation or visiting busy markets, solo travelers should remain vigilant and be aware of their belongings at all times.

Staying connected with friends and family back home is another important aspect of solo travel safety. Regularly updating loved ones on travel plans, whereabouts, and any changes to the itinerary can provide peace of mind and ensure that someone is aware of the traveler's movements. Sharing accommodation details and emergency contact information with a trusted person can also be beneficial in case of any unexpected situations. Solo travelers should consider using messaging apps or social media to stay in touch, as well as having a local SIM card or an international phone plan to maintain reliable communication.

Navigating transportation on the Amalfi Coast can be a unique experience, and solo travelers should be aware of the available options and safety considerations. The region is known for its narrow, winding roads and picturesque but challenging driving conditions. While renting a car can offer flexibility and convenience, it may not be the best option for all travelers, especially those who are not comfortable driving in unfamiliar terrain. Public transportation, including buses and ferries, is a popular and reliable way to travel between towns. It is important to check schedules in advance, as services can vary depending on the season and time of day. When using taxis or ride-sharing services, solo travelers should use licensed and reputable providers and avoid accepting rides from unmarked or unofficial vehicles.

Exploring the Amalfi Coast on foot is a rewarding and enjoyable experience, but solo travelers should take certain precautions to ensure their safety. Wearing comfortable and appropriate footwear is essential, as the terrain can be steep and uneven in places. Staying hydrated and carrying a water bottle is also important, particularly during the warmer months. It is advisable to stick to well-marked paths and avoid wandering into isolated or unfamiliar areas, especially after dark. Solo travelers should also be cautious when hiking or visiting remote locations and consider joining guided tours or group excursions for added safety and companionship.

Solo travelers should be mindful of personal safety and take steps to avoid potentially risky situations. Trusting one's instincts and avoiding situations or individuals that feel uncomfortable or unsafe is crucial. It is important to remain aware of one's surroundings and avoid excessive alcohol consumption, which can impair judgment and increase vulnerability. Solo travelers should also be cautious when accepting food or drinks from strangers and ensure that their drinks are never left unattended.

Understanding and respecting local customs and etiquette can also contribute to a safe and positive travel experience. Italians are known for their warm hospitality, but solo travelers should be aware of cultural norms and practices to avoid misunderstandings or offense. Dressing modestly when visiting religious sites, using polite language, and observing social customs can help solo travelers blend in and show respect for the local culture. Learning a few basic Italian phrases can also be helpful in navigating interactions and showing appreciation for the local language.

In addition to these practical safety tips, solo travelers should prioritize their health and well-being while on the Amalfi Coast. Carrying a basic first aid kit and any necessary medications can be important in case of minor injuries or illnesses. It is also advisable to have travel insurance that covers medical expenses, emergency evacuation, and trip cancellations. Staying informed about local health guidelines and recommendations, particularly in the context of ongoing global health concerns, can help solo travelers stay safe and healthy during their trip.

Another important aspect of solo travel safety is managing money and finances wisely. Solo travelers should carry a mix of cash and credit cards and be aware of the locations of ATMs and banks. It is advisable to avoid carrying large amounts of cash and to use credit cards for larger purchases whenever possible. Keeping a separate stash of emergency cash in a secure location, such as a hidden pocket or a locked suitcase, can provide a backup in case of theft or loss. Solo travelers should also be cautious when using public Wi-Fi for online banking or financial transactions and consider using a VPN to protect their information.

Finally, solo travelers should take the time to enjoy their journey and embrace the unique experiences that the Amalfi Coast has to offer. While safety is a priority, it is also important to remain open to new adventures and connections. Joining group activities, participating in local events, and engaging with fellow travelers and locals can enhance the travel experience and create lasting memories. Solo travel on the Amalfi Coast can be a deeply rewarding and transformative experience, offering the opportunity for personal growth, cultural immersion, and unforgettable moments.

The Amalfi Coast is a beautiful and captivating destination that offers a wealth of experiences for solo travelers. By following these safety tips and being mindful of their surroundings, solo travelers can ensure a safe and enjoyable trip. Thorough planning, choosing the right accommodation, staying connected with loved ones, being cautious with transportation and personal safety, respecting local customs, prioritizing health and well-being, managing finances wisely, and embracing the adventure are all key components of a successful solo journey on the Amalfi Coast. With the right preparation and mindset, solo travelers can explore this stunning region with confidence and create cherished memories that will last a lifetime.

Top Destinations for Solo Explorers

The Amalfi Coast is one of the most picturesque and culturally rich destinations in Italy, offering a variety of experiences for solo travelers. With its dramatic cliffs, azure waters, charming towns, and historical sites, the region provides a perfect blend of natural beauty and cultural heritage. For solo explorers, the Amalfi Coast offers the freedom to wander at their own pace and the opportunity to immerse themselves fully in the local atmosphere. This detailed guide will provide an in-depth look at the top destinations on the Amalfi Coast for solo travelers, ensuring a comprehensive understanding of what each location has to offer.

One of the most iconic destinations on the Amalfi Coast is the town of Positano. Known for its colorful buildings cascading down the cliffs to the sea, Positano is a vibrant and lively town that captures the essence of the Amalfi Coast. For solo travelers, Positano offers a variety of experiences, from exploring narrow streets filled with boutiques and cafes to relaxing on the beautiful Spiaggia Grande beach. The town is also home to several historical sites, such as the Church of Santa Maria Assunta, which features a stunning Byzantine icon of the Black Madonna. Solo travelers can enjoy wandering through the town, taking in the views, and sampling local delicacies such as fresh seafood and lemon desserts. The friendly and welcoming atmosphere of Positano makes it an ideal destination for solo exploration.

Another must-visit destination is Amalfi, the town that gives the coast its name. Amalfi is rich in history and culture, having been a powerful maritime republic in the Middle Ages. The town's most famous landmark is the Amalfi Cathedral, a stunning example of medieval architecture with its striking facade and intricate interior. The cathedral houses the remains of Saint Andrew, the patron saint of Amalfi, and is a significant pilgrimage site. Solo travelers can explore the cathedral, wander through the charming streets of the town, and visit the nearby Paper Museum (Museo della Carta), which showcases the traditional paper-making techniques that have been used in Amalfi for centuries. The town's picturesque harbor and seaside promenade offer beautiful views and a relaxed atmosphere for solo explorers.

Ravello, perched high above the coast, is another top destination for solo travelers. Known for its breathtaking views and beautiful gardens, Ravello has long been a haven for artists, writers, and musicians. The town is home to the stunning Villa Rufolo and Villa Cimbrone, both of which feature exquisite gardens and panoramic views of the coastline. The Terrace of Infinity at Villa Cimbrone is particularly famous for its dramatic and sweeping vistas. Solo travelers can spend hours wandering through the gardens, taking in the scenery, and enjoying the peaceful ambiance. Ravello is also known for its cultural events, including the Ravello Festival, which features classical music concerts in the open-air gardens. The town's artistic and tranquil atmosphere makes it a perfect destination for solo travelers seeking inspiration and solitude.

For a more off-the-beaten-path experience, solo travelers should consider visiting the town of Atrani. Located just a short distance from Amalfi, Atrani is one of the smallest and most picturesque towns on the coast. Its narrow streets, archways, and small squares create a charming and intimate atmosphere. Atrani's main square, Piazza Umberto I, is a great place to relax and enjoy a coffee or gelato while watching the local life. The town is also home to the Church of San Salvatore de' Birecto, an ancient church with beautiful frescoes and a peaceful interior. Atrani's quiet and authentic charm makes it a hidden gem for solo travelers looking to escape the more crowded tourist spots.

Maiori, with its long sandy beach and relaxed vibe, is another excellent destination for solo travelers. The town offers a variety of activities, from lounging on the beach to exploring historical sites such as the Castle of San Nicola de Thoro-Plano, a medieval fortress with panoramic views. Solo travelers can also visit the nearby Abbey of Santa Maria de Olearia, an ancient monastery with beautiful frescoes. Maiori's wide promenade is perfect for a leisurely stroll, and the town's numerous cafes and restaurants offer plenty of opportunities to sample local cuisine. The friendly and laid-back atmosphere of Maiori makes it an inviting destination for solo travelers.

Minori, known as the "City of Taste," is a paradise for food lovers. The town is famous for its traditional pasta, particularly the hand-rolled "ndunderi," which is said to date back to Roman times. Solo travelers can visit the local pasta shops and bakeries to sample these delicious treats. Minori is also home to the Villa Romana, an ancient Roman villa with well-preserved mosaics and frescoes. The town's lemon groves and terraced vineyards add to its charm, and solo travelers can enjoy peaceful walks through the countryside.

Minori's focus on food and tradition makes it a delightful destination for solo travelers seeking a culinary adventure.

For solo travelers who enjoy hiking and nature, the Path of the Gods (Sentiero degli Dei) is a must-do experience. This famous hiking trail runs from the village of Bomerano in Agerola to Nocelle, a hamlet above Positano. The trail offers spectacular views of the coastline, the sea, and the surrounding mountains. Solo travelers can take their time to explore the trail, stopping to enjoy the scenery and take photographs. The hike is moderately challenging and well-marked, making it suitable for hikers of various levels. The sense of accomplishment and the stunning vistas make the Path of the Gods a memorable experience for solo travelers.

Praiano, a quieter and more laid-back town, is another great destination for solo travelers. Praiano offers beautiful beaches, such as Marina di Praia and Gavitella Beach, as well as several charming churches, including the Church of San Gennaro, which features a beautiful tiled dome. The town is also known for its stunning sunsets, which can be enjoyed from various viewpoints along the coast. Solo travelers can explore the town's narrow streets, relax on the beach, and enjoy the peaceful ambiance. Praiano's unspoiled charm and tranquility make it an ideal destination for solo travelers looking for a more serene experience.

The island of Capri, located just off the coast, is another top destination for solo travelers. Known for its rugged landscape, upscale shops, and stunning views, Capri offers a variety of experiences. Solo travelers can take a boat tour around the island to visit the famous Blue Grotto, a sea cave with mesmerizing blue waters. The island is also home to the town of Anacapri, which offers a more laid-back atmosphere and beautiful views from Monte Solaro, the highest point on the island. Capri's charming streets, luxury boutiques, and natural beauty make it a captivating destination for solo travelers.

In addition to these specific destinations, solo travelers on the Amalfi Coast should take advantage of the region's excellent public transportation options, including buses and ferries, which make it easy to explore multiple towns and attractions. The SITA bus service connects the major towns along the coast, while ferries offer scenic and convenient travel between coastal towns and nearby islands.

The Amalfi Coast offers a wealth of destinations and experiences for solo travelers. From the vibrant and picturesque town of Positano to the historical and cultural richness of Amalfi and the artistic charm of Ravello, each location provides its own unique appeal. Smaller towns like Atrani and Praiano offer a more intimate and tranquil experience, while destinations like Maiori and Minori cater to food lovers and beachgoers. The island of Capri adds another dimension to the Amalfi Coast experience, with its stunning landscapes and luxury offerings. By exploring these top destinations, solo travelers can immerse themselves in the beauty and culture of the Amalfi Coast, creating unforgettable memories and experiences.

Solo-Friendly Activities and Tours

The Amalfi Coast, renowned for its stunning scenery, historical richness, and vibrant culture, is a perfect destination for solo travelers seeking unique and enriching experiences. The region offers a variety of activities and tours that cater specifically to individuals exploring on their own. From guided tours and hiking trails to culinary classes and cultural workshops, there is an abundance of solo-friendly activities that allow travelers to immerse themselves in the beauty and culture of the Amalfi Coast. This detailed guide will provide an extensive overview of the best solo-friendly activities and tours, ensuring a comprehensive and informative understanding for anyone planning to visit this enchanting part of Italy.

One of the most rewarding solo-friendly activities on the Amalfi Coast is joining guided tours. These tours provide an excellent way to explore the region while gaining insights from knowledgeable guides. One highly recommended tour is the Amalfi Coast Full-Day Tour, which typically includes visits to iconic towns such as Positano, Amalfi, and Ravello. This tour allows solo travelers to experience the highlights of the coast, including historical sites, beautiful landscapes, and local culture. The guides often share fascinating stories and historical context, enhancing the overall experience and providing a deeper appreciation for the region.

For solo travelers interested in history and culture, a tour of the ancient ruins of Pompeii is a must. The Pompeii and Amalfi Coast Day Trip combines a visit to the well-preserved ruins of Pompeii with an exploration of the Amalfi Coast. In Pompeii, solo travelers can join a guided tour to learn about the daily life of the ancient Romans and the catastrophic eruption of Mount Vesuvius that buried the city. This tour provides a unique opportunity to walk through the streets of Pompeii, see the remains of houses, temples, and public buildings, and gain a vivid understanding of ancient Roman civilization. Following the visit to Pompeii, the tour continues along the scenic Amalfi Coast, offering breathtaking views and the chance to explore charming coastal towns.

Another excellent solo-friendly tour is the Capri Day Trip from the Amalfi Coast. This tour includes a boat trip to the island of Capri, known for its rugged coastline, luxury shops, and natural beauty. Solo travelers can enjoy a guided boat tour around the island, visiting famous sites such as the Blue Grotto, a sea cave with stunning blue waters. On the island, the tour often includes a visit to Anacapri, a quieter town with beautiful views from Monte Solaro, the highest point on the island. This day trip provides a perfect blend of natural beauty and cultural exploration, making it an ideal choice for solo travelers.

For those who enjoy nature and outdoor activities, hiking on the Amalfi Coast offers a range of solo-friendly options. The Path of the Gods (Sentiero degli Dei) is one of the most famous hiking trails in the region. This trail runs from Bomerano to Nocelle, offering spectacular views of the coastline and the Mediterranean Sea. Solo travelers can take their time to explore the trail, enjoying the stunning scenery and the sense of tranquility. The Path of the Gods is well-marked and suitable for hikers of various levels, making it a popular choice for solo adventurers. Along the way, hikers pass through terraced vineyards, ancient ruins, and charming villages, providing a diverse and enriching experience.

Another fantastic hiking option is the Valle delle Ferriere trail, which takes hikers through a lush nature reserve near Amalfi. This trail offers a peaceful escape into nature, with dense forests, cascading waterfalls, and rare plants. The Valle delle Ferriere is known for its unique microclimate, which supports a variety of plant species not found elsewhere in the region. Solo travelers can enjoy the serene atmosphere and the opportunity to connect with nature. The trail also includes the remains of ancient ironworks, adding a historical dimension to the hike.

For a more leisurely outdoor activity, solo travelers can explore the coastal towns and villages on foot. Towns such as Positano, Amalfi, and Ravello are perfect for solo exploration, with their narrow streets, picturesque squares, and stunning views. In Positano, solo travelers can wander through the town's colorful streets, visit the Church of Santa Maria Assunta, and relax on the Spiaggia Grande beach. Amalfi offers historical sites such as the Amalfi Cathedral and the Paper Museum, as well as a beautiful harbor and seaside promenade. Ravello is known for its exquisite gardens at Villa Rufolo and Villa Cimbrone, as well as its cultural events, including the Ravello Festival. Exploring these towns on foot allows solo travelers to soak in the local atmosphere and discover hidden gems at their own pace.

Culinary experiences are another highlight of solo travel on the Amalfi Coast. Food and wine tours provide an opportunity to sample the region's delicious cuisine and learn about its culinary traditions. The Amalfi Coast Food and Wine Tour is a popular choice, combining visits to local vineyards, olive groves, and food producers with tastings of regional specialties. Solo travelers can sample local wines, olive oils, cheeses, and cured meats, gaining a deeper understanding of the region's culinary heritage. The tour often includes a visit to a traditional limoncello producer, where participants can learn about the production process and taste this iconic lemon liqueur.

Cooking classes are another excellent solo-friendly activity, offering a hands-on introduction to Amalfi Coast cuisine. Many cooking schools and local chefs offer classes that teach participants how to prepare traditional dishes using fresh, local ingredients. These classes often include a visit to a local market to select ingredients, followed by a hands-on cooking session and a shared meal. Solo travelers can enjoy the opportunity to learn new skills, meet other travelers, and savor the delicious results of their efforts. One notable option is Mamma Agata's Cooking School in Ravello, which offers a warm and welcoming environment and teaches participants to prepare a variety of traditional dishes.

Art and craft workshops provide another enriching activity for solo travelers. The Amalfi Coast is known for its ceramics, paper-making, and textiles, and many local artisans offer workshops and classes where visitors can learn these traditional crafts. In Vietri sul Mare, solo travelers can join a ceramics workshop to learn about the techniques and traditions of this craft and create their own hand-painted pieces. In Amalfi, the Paper Museum offers classes in traditional paper-making, allowing participants to create beautiful handmade paper using centuries-old methods. These workshops provide a unique and hands-on way to connect with the region's artistic heritage and create meaningful souvenirs.

For solo travelers seeking relaxation and rejuvenation, wellness and spa experiences are abundant on the Amalfi Coast. Many hotels and wellness centers offer a range of treatments, from massages and facials to holistic therapies and yoga sessions. The Monastero Santa Rosa Hotel & Spa, perched on a cliff above the sea, offers a luxurious and serene retreat with a range of wellness treatments. Solo travelers can enjoy the thermal suite, hydrotherapy pool, and a variety of spa treatments, all while taking in the stunning views of the coastline. The Caruso, A Belmond Hotel, in Ravello, also offers a world-class spa with indoor and outdoor treatment rooms, providing a perfect setting for relaxation and self-care.

Boat tours and cruises offer another fantastic way for solo travelers to explore the Amalfi Coast. These tours provide a different perspective on the region's stunning coastline and allow participants to visit hidden coves, sea caves, and picturesque villages that are often difficult to reach by land. One popular option is a sunset cruise, which offers the chance to enjoy the beautiful colors of the sunset while cruising along the coast. Many boat tours also include stops at key attractions, such as the Grotta dello Smeraldo and the island of Capri. For a more personalized experience, solo travelers can rent a small boat or join a private tour, allowing them to explore the coastline at their own pace.

The Amalfi Coast offers a wealth of solo-friendly activities and tours that cater to a variety of interests and preferences. From guided tours and hiking trails to culinary classes and wellness experiences, there are countless ways for solo travelers to explore and enjoy this stunning region. By engaging in these activities, solo travelers can immerse themselves in the beauty, culture, and traditions of the Amalfi Coast, creating unforgettable memories and enriching their travel experience. Whether you are seeking adventure, relaxation, or cultural enrichment, the Amalfi

Coast provides a diverse and rewarding array of solo-friendly experiences that are sure to leave a lasting impression.

CHAPTER 10

TRAVELING AS A COUPLE

Romantic Spots and Experiences

The Amalfi Coast is renowned for its breathtaking scenery, charming towns, and romantic atmosphere, making it an ideal destination for couples. This stunning region offers a wealth of romantic spots and experiences that cater to all tastes and preferences. Whether you are looking for intimate moments, scenic views, or luxurious experiences, the Amalfi Coast has something to offer every couple.

One of the most iconic and romantic destinations on the Amalfi Coast is the town of Positano. Known for its colorful buildings cascading down the cliffs to the sea, Positano offers a magical setting for couples. The narrow streets, lined with boutiques, cafes, and art galleries, are perfect for leisurely strolls hand-in-hand. The town's main beach, Spiaggia Grande, provides a beautiful backdrop for relaxing by the sea, and the beachside bars and restaurants offer the perfect setting for a romantic meal with a view. One of the most romantic experiences in Positano is dining at a seaside restaurant, such as Ristorante La Sponda, where the twinkling lights and sea breeze create an unforgettable ambiance.

Amalfi, with its rich history and picturesque setting, is another top destination for couples. The town's charming streets, historic sites, and stunning views make it an ideal place for romantic exploration. A visit to the Amalfi Cathedral, with its striking facade and beautiful interior, provides a unique and intimate experience. Couples can also explore the town's many shops and cafes, enjoying the relaxed and welcoming atmosphere. A romantic walk along the seaside promenade, taking in the views of the harbor and the sea, is a must-do activity in Amalfi. The town's many restaurants, such as Ristorante Eolo, offer the perfect setting for a romantic dinner, with delicious cuisine and stunning views.

Ravello, perched high above the coast, is known for its breathtaking views and beautiful gardens, making it a perfect destination for couples. The town's main attractions, Villa Rufolo and Villa Cimbrone, offer some of the most romantic settings on the Amalfi Coast. The gardens of Villa Rufolo, with their exotic plants and stunning views, provide a peaceful and intimate setting for a romantic stroll. The Terrace of Infinity at Villa Cimbrone offers one of the most breathtaking views in Italy, with a sweeping panorama of the coastline and the sea. Couples can enjoy the serene atmosphere and the stunning scenery, creating unforgettable memories. Ravello is also known for its cultural events, such as the Ravello Festival, which features classical music concerts in the open-air gardens, providing a unique and romantic experience.

For a more secluded and intimate experience, the town of Atrani is a hidden gem on the Amalfi Coast. Located just a short distance from Amalfi, Atrani is one of the smallest and most picturesque towns in the region. Its narrow streets, archways, and small squares create a charming and intimate atmosphere, perfect for couples seeking a quiet and romantic escape. The town's main square, Piazza Umberto I, is a great place to relax and enjoy a coffee or gelato while watching the local life. Atrani's quiet and authentic charm makes it a hidden gem for couples looking to escape the more crowded tourist spots.

Maiori, with its long sandy beach and relaxed vibe, is another excellent destination for couples. The town offers a variety of activities, from lounging on the beach to exploring historical sites such as the Castle of San Nicola de Thoro-Plano, a medieval fortress with panoramic views. Couples can also visit the nearby Abbey of Santa Maria de Olearia, an ancient monastery with beautiful frescoes. Maiori's wide promenade is perfect for a leisurely stroll, and the town's numerous cafes and restaurants offer plenty of opportunities to sample local cuisine. The friendly and laid-back atmosphere of Maiori makes it an inviting destination for couples.

Minori, known as the "City of Taste," is a paradise for food lovers. The town is famous for its traditional pasta, particularly the hand-rolled "ndunderi," which is said to date back to Roman times. Couples can visit the local pasta shops and bakeries to sample these delicious treats. Minori is also home to the Villa Romana, an ancient Roman villa with well-preserved mosaics and frescoes. The town's lemon groves and terraced vineyards add to its charm, and couples can enjoy peaceful walks through the countryside. Minori's focus on food and tradition makes it a delightful destination for couples seeking a culinary adventure.

For couples who enjoy hiking and nature, the Path of the Gods (Sentiero degli Dei) is a must-do experience. This famous hiking trail runs from the village of Bomerano in Agerola to Nocelle, a hamlet above Positano. The trail offers spectacular views of the coastline, the sea, and the surrounding mountains. Couples can take their time to explore the trail, enjoying the stunning scenery and the sense of tranquility. The Path of the Gods is well-marked and suitable for hikers of various levels, making it a popular choice for couples who enjoy outdoor activities. Along the way, hikers pass through terraced vineyards, ancient ruins, and charming villages, providing a diverse and enriching experience.

Praiano, a quieter and more laid-back town, is another great destination for couples. Praiano offers beautiful beaches, such as Marina di Praia and Gavitella Beach, as well as several charming churches, including the Church of San Gennaro, which features a beautiful tiled dome. The town is also known for its stunning sunsets, which can be enjoyed from various viewpoints along the coast. Couples can explore the town's narrow streets, relax on the beach, and enjoy the peaceful ambiance. Praiano's unspoiled charm and tranquility make it an ideal destination for couples looking for a more serene experience.

The island of Capri, located just off the coast, is another top destination for couples. Known for its rugged landscape, upscale shops, and stunning views, Capri offers a variety of experiences. Couples can take a boat tour around the island to visit the famous Blue Grotto, a sea cave with mesmerizing blue waters. On the island, a visit to Anacapri offers a more laid-back atmosphere and beautiful views from Monte Solaro, the highest point on the island. Capri's charming streets, luxury boutiques, and natural beauty make it a captivating destination for couples.

In addition to these specific destinations, couples on the Amalfi Coast should take advantage of the region's excellent public transportation options, including buses and ferries, which make it easy to explore multiple towns and attractions. The SITA bus service connects the major towns along the coast, while ferries offer scenic and convenient travel between coastal towns and nearby islands.

The Amalfi Coast offers a wealth of romantic spots and experiences for couples. From the vibrant and picturesque town of Positano to the historical and cultural richness of Amalfi and the artistic charm of Ravello, each location provides its own unique appeal. Smaller towns like Atrani and Praiano offer a more intimate and tranquil experience, while destinations like Maiori and Minori cater to food lovers and beachgoers. The island of Capri adds another dimension to the Amalfi Coast experience, with its stunning landscapes and luxury offerings. By exploring these top destinations, couples can immerse themselves in the beauty and culture of the Amalfi Coast, creating unforgettable memories and experiences.

Best Date Night Restaurants

The Amalfi Coast, known for its stunning views, rich history, and vibrant culture, also boasts some of the most romantic dining spots in Italy. Couples seeking a memorable date night will find a plethora of restaurants that offer not just exquisite cuisine but also enchanting atmospheres that are perfect for a romantic evening.

One of the most celebrated restaurants for a romantic date night is Ristorante La Sponda in Positano. Located in the renowned Le Sirenuse Hotel, this restaurant is famous for its breathtaking views of the town and the sea, especially when illuminated at night. The restaurant's interior is equally enchanting, with candlelit tables and an abundance of greenery creating a magical ambiance. La Sponda offers a menu that highlights traditional Mediterranean flavors with a modern twist, using fresh, local ingredients. Dishes such as homemade pasta, fresh seafood, and decadent desserts are beautifully presented and paired with an extensive wine list.

The impeccable service and stunning setting make La Sponda an unforgettable dining experience for couples.

Another top choice for a romantic dinner is Ristorante Eolo in Amalfi. Perched on a cliff overlooking the sea, Eolo provides a picturesque setting with panoramic views of the coastline. The restaurant features a charming terrace where couples can dine al fresco while enjoying the gentle sea breeze and the sound of the waves. Eolo's menu focuses on contemporary Italian cuisine with an emphasis on fresh seafood and locally sourced produce. Signature dishes include grilled octopus, lemon-infused risotto, and a variety of delectable desserts. The combination of exquisite food, attentive service, and a romantic setting makes Ristorante Eolo a perfect choice for a memorable date night.

In Ravello, Ristorante Rossellinis at the Palazzo Avino offers an elegant and intimate dining experience. The restaurant's terrace provides stunning views of the Amalfi Coast, making it an ideal spot for a romantic evening. Rossellinis is known for its refined Italian cuisine, featuring dishes that showcase the best of local ingredients and culinary traditions. The menu includes a variety of appetizers, pasta dishes, and main courses, all expertly prepared and presented. Couples can enjoy a tasting menu that allows them to sample a range of flavors and textures, complemented by a carefully curated wine list. The sophisticated ambiance and exceptional cuisine make Rossellinis a top choice for a special night out.

For a truly unique and romantic dining experience, couples can visit Il Refettorio at the Monastero Santa Rosa Hotel & Spa in Conca dei Marini. Housed in a former monastery, the restaurant offers a serene and historic setting with beautiful views of the sea. The dining room features vaulted ceilings and elegant decor, creating a sophisticated yet intimate atmosphere. Il Refettorio's menu is inspired by the flavors of the Amalfi Coast, with a focus on fresh, seasonal ingredients. Dishes such as handmade pasta, locally caught fish, and traditional desserts are crafted with care and creativity. The exceptional service and tranquil setting make Il Refettorio an ideal choice for a romantic dinner.

In Positano, Da Adolfo offers a more relaxed and intimate dining experience that is perfect for couples looking to enjoy a casual yet memorable evening. Located on a small beach accessible by boat, Da Adolfo provides a unique and charming setting. The restaurant's rustic decor and beachfront location create a laid-back and romantic atmosphere. The menu features a variety of fresh seafood dishes, including grilled fish, seafood pasta, and a famous mozzarella grilled on lemon leaves. Couples can dine under the stars, with the sound of the waves providing a soothing backdrop. The combination of delicious food and a unique setting makes Da Adolfo a standout choice for a romantic evening.

La Tagliata in Montepertuso, a small village above Positano, offers a warm and welcoming atmosphere that is perfect for a romantic dinner. The family-run restaurant is known for its hearty Italian cuisine and stunning views of the coast. The dining room features rustic decor and a cozy ambiance, while the outdoor terrace provides a beautiful setting for al fresco dining. La Tagliata's menu is based on traditional recipes and locally sourced ingredients, with dishes such as homemade pasta, grilled meats, and fresh vegetables. The generous portions and friendly service make La Tagliata a great choice for couples looking for an authentic and memorable dining experience.

For couples seeking a luxurious and elegant dining experience, Terrazza Bosquet at the Grand Hotel Excelsior Vittoria in Sorrento is an excellent choice. The restaurant offers stunning views of the Bay of Naples and Mount Vesuvius, providing a breathtaking backdrop for a romantic dinner. The menu features a blend of traditional and contemporary Italian cuisine, with dishes crafted from the finest local ingredients. Couples can enjoy a multi-course tasting menu that showcases the chef's creativity and skill, complemented by an extensive wine list. The refined ambiance and exceptional cuisine make Terrazza Bosquet a perfect destination for a special night out.

In Amalfi, Marina Grande offers a chic and contemporary dining experience with a focus on fresh seafood and Mediterranean flavors. The restaurant is located on the beach, providing a beautiful setting for a romantic dinner. The modern decor and elegant ambiance create a sophisticated yet relaxed atmosphere. Marina Grande's menu features a variety of seafood dishes, including crudo, pasta with seafood, and grilled fish, all prepared with care and creativity. The extensive wine list and attentive service add to the overall experience, making Marina Grande a top choice for a romantic evening.

Le Sirenuse in Positano is another excellent option for couples seeking a romantic dining experience. The restaurant offers stunning views of the town and the sea, creating a magical setting for a special night out. The menu features traditional Italian cuisine with a contemporary twist, using fresh, local ingredients. Dishes such as homemade pasta, fresh seafood, and decadent desserts are beautifully presented and paired with an extensive wine list. The impeccable service and stunning setting make Le Sirenuse an unforgettable dining experience for couples.

In Ravello, the Belmond Hotel Caruso's restaurant, Belvedere, offers a luxurious and romantic dining experience. The restaurant's terrace provides stunning views of the Amalfi Coast, making it an ideal spot for a romantic evening. Belvedere is known for its refined Italian cuisine, featuring dishes that showcase the best of local ingredients and culinary traditions. The menu includes a variety of appetizers, pasta dishes, and main courses, all expertly prepared and presented. Couples can enjoy a tasting menu that allows them to sample a range of flavors and textures, complemented by a carefully curated wine list. The sophisticated ambiance and exceptional cuisine make Belvedere a top choice for a special night out.

For a truly unique and romantic dining experience, couples can visit Il San Pietro di Positano's restaurant, Zass. Housed in a stunning cliffside setting, the restaurant offers breathtaking views of the sea and the surrounding coastline. The dining room features elegant decor and a refined atmosphere, creating a sophisticated yet intimate setting. Zass's menu is inspired by the flavors of the Amalfi Coast, with a focus on fresh, seasonal ingredients. Dishes such as handmade pasta, locally caught fish, and traditional desserts are crafted with care and creativity. The exceptional service and tranquil setting make Zass an ideal choice for a romantic dinner.

The Amalfi Coast offers a wealth of romantic dining options for couples. From the elegant and refined settings of Ristorante La Sponda and Ristorante Eolo to the more relaxed and intimate atmospheres of Da Adolfo and La Tagliata, there is something to suit every taste and preference. Each restaurant provides a unique and memorable experience, with stunning views, exquisite cuisine, and exceptional service. By exploring these top date night restaurants, couples can create unforgettable memories and enjoy the best of what the Amalfi Coast has to offer. Whether you are celebrating a special occasion or simply enjoying a night out, the Amalfi Coast provides the perfect backdrop for a romantic and memorable dining experience.

Couples' Activities and Tours

The Amalfi Coast, with its dramatic landscapes, picturesque towns, and rich cultural heritage, offers an ideal setting for couples seeking a romantic and memorable getaway. The region is filled with activities and tours that cater specifically to couples, providing opportunities for shared experiences that can strengthen bonds and create lasting memories.

One of the most romantic activities for couples on the Amalfi Coast is taking a boat tour. The coastline is best appreciated from the sea, where couples can enjoy breathtaking views of the cliffs, beaches, and charming towns. Private boat tours offer an intimate and personalized experience, with options ranging from half-day excursions to full-day adventures. These tours often include stops at hidden coves and secluded beaches, where couples can swim and relax in privacy. A popular choice is a sunset cruise, where couples can watch the sun set over the Mediterranean Sea while sipping on a glass of Prosecco. Many tours also offer the option to visit the famous Blue Grotto on the island of Capri, a sea cave known for its stunning blue light.

For couples who enjoy exploring on foot, the Path of the Gods (Sentiero degli Dei) is a must-do experience. This famous hiking trail runs from the village of Bomerano in Agerola to Nocelle, a hamlet above Positano. The trail offers spectacular views of the coastline, the sea, and the surrounding mountains. Couples can take their time to explore the trail, enjoying the stunning scenery and the sense of tranquility. The Path of the Gods is well-marked and suitable for hikers of various levels, making it a popular choice for couples who enjoy outdoor activities. Along the way, hikers pass through terraced vineyards, ancient ruins, and charming villages, providing a diverse and enriching experience.

Exploring the picturesque towns of the Amalfi Coast is another romantic activity that couples can enjoy together. Positano, with its colorful buildings and narrow streets, is a favorite destination for couples. The town's main beach, Spiaggia Grande, provides a beautiful backdrop for relaxing by the sea, and the beachside bars and restaurants offer the perfect setting for a romantic meal with a view. Couples can also wander through the town's boutiques and art galleries, discovering unique souvenirs and local crafts. Another highlight is a visit to the Church of Santa Maria Assunta, which features a stunning Byzantine icon of the Black Madonna.

Amalfi, with its rich history and picturesque setting, is another top destination for couples. The town's charming streets, historic sites, and stunning views make it an ideal place for romantic exploration. A visit to the Amalfi Cathedral, with its striking facade and beautiful interior, provides a unique and intimate experience. Couples can also explore the town's many shops and cafes, enjoying the relaxed and welcoming atmosphere. A romantic walk along the seaside promenade, taking in the views of the harbor and the sea, is a must-do activity in Amalfi. The town's many restaurants, such as Ristorante Eolo, offer the perfect setting for a romantic dinner, with delicious cuisine and stunning views.

Ravello, perched high above the coast, is known for its breathtaking views and beautiful gardens, making it a perfect destination for couples. The town's main attractions, Villa Rufolo and Villa Cimbrone, offer some of the most romantic settings on the Amalfi Coast. The gardens of Villa Rufolo, with their exotic plants and stunning views, provide a peaceful and intimate setting for a romantic stroll. The Terrace of Infinity at Villa Cimbrone offers one of the most breathtaking views in Italy, with a sweeping panorama of the coastline and the sea. Couples can enjoy the serene atmosphere and the stunning scenery, creating unforgettable memories. Ravello is also known for its cultural events, such as the Ravello Festival, which features classical music concerts in the open-air gardens, providing a unique and romantic experience.

For a more secluded and intimate experience, the town of Atrani is a hidden gem on the Amalfi Coast. Located just a short distance from Amalfi, Atrani is one of the smallest and most picturesque towns in the region. Its narrow streets, archways, and small squares create a charming and intimate atmosphere, perfect for couples seeking a quiet and romantic escape. The town's main square, Piazza Umberto I, is a great place to relax and enjoy a coffee or gelato while watching the local life. Atrani's quiet and authentic charm makes it a hidden gem for couples looking to escape the more crowded tourist spots.

Maiori, with its long sandy beach and relaxed vibe, is another excellent destination for couples. The town offers a variety of activities, from lounging on the beach to exploring historical sites such as the Castle of San Nicola de Thoro-Plano, a medieval fortress with panoramic views. Couples can also visit the nearby Abbey of Santa Maria de Olearia, an ancient monastery with beautiful frescoes. Maiori's wide promenade is perfect for a leisurely stroll, and the town's numerous cafes and restaurants offer plenty of opportunities to sample local cuisine. The friendly and laid-back atmosphere of Maiori makes it an inviting destination for couples.

Minori, known as the "City of Taste," is a paradise for food lovers. The town is famous for its traditional pasta, particularly the hand-rolled "ndunderi," which is said to date back to Roman times. Couples can visit the local pasta shops and bakeries to sample these delicious treats. Minori is also home to the Villa Romana, an ancient Roman villa with well-preserved mosaics and frescoes. The town's lemon groves and terraced vineyards add to its charm, and couples can enjoy peaceful walks through the countryside. Minori's focus on food and tradition makes it a delightful destination for couples seeking a culinary adventure.

For couples who enjoy wine, a visit to a local vineyard is a must. The Amalfi Coast is home to several vineyards that produce excellent wines, particularly whites and rosés. Couples can take a guided tour of the vineyards, learning about the wine-making process and sampling a variety of wines. Many tours also include a visit to the cellar and a tasting of local products such as olive oil and cheese. One of the most renowned vineyards in the region is Marisa Cuomo, located in the town of Furore. The vineyard offers guided tours and tastings, providing couples with a unique and memorable experience.

Cooking classes are another excellent activity for couples on the Amalfi Coast. Many cooking schools and local chefs offer classes that teach participants how to prepare traditional dishes using fresh, local ingredients. These classes often include a visit to a local market to select ingredients, followed by a hands-on cooking session and a shared meal. Couples can enjoy the opportunity to learn new skills, meet other travelers, and savor the delicious results of their efforts. One notable option is Mamma Agata's Cooking School in Ravello, which offers a warm and welcoming environment and teaches participants to prepare a variety of traditional dishes.

Art and craft workshops provide another enriching activity for couples. The Amalfi Coast is known for its ceramics, paper-making, and textiles, and many local artisans offer workshops and classes where visitors can learn these traditional crafts. In Vietri sul Mare, couples can join a ceramics workshop to learn about the techniques and traditions of this craft and create their own hand-painted pieces. In Amalfi, the Paper Museum offers classes in traditional paper-making, allowing participants to create beautiful handmade paper using centuries-old methods. These workshops provide a unique and hands-on way to connect with the region's artistic heritage and create meaningful souvenirs.

Wellness and spa experiences are abundant on the Amalfi Coast, providing couples with the perfect opportunity to relax and rejuvenate together. Many hotels and wellness centers offer a range of treatments, from massages and facials to holistic therapies and yoga sessions. The Monastero Santa Rosa Hotel & Spa, perched on a cliff above the sea, offers a luxurious and serene retreat with a range of wellness treatments. Couples can enjoy the thermal suite, hydrotherapy pool, and a variety of spa treatments, all while taking in the stunning views of the coastline. The Caruso, A Belmond Hotel, in Ravello, also offers a world-class spa with indoor and outdoor treatment rooms, providing a perfect setting for relaxation and self-care.

The Amalfi Coast offers a wealth of activities and tours that are perfect for couples. From boat tours and hiking trails to exploring picturesque towns and enjoying culinary experiences, there are countless ways for couples to create unforgettable memories together. Each activity provides a unique and enriching experience, allowing couples to immerse themselves in the beauty, culture, and traditions of the Amalfi Coast. Whether you are seeking adventure, relaxation, or cultural enrichment, the Amalfi Coast provides the perfect backdrop for a romantic and memorable getaway.

Honeymoon and Anniversary Ideas

The Amalfi Coast is one of the most romantic and picturesque destinations in the world, making it an ideal place for honeymoons and anniversaries. Its stunning landscapes, charming towns, and rich cultural heritage provide the perfect backdrop for celebrating love and creating unforgettable memories. From luxurious accommodations and fine dining to intimate experiences and adventurous activities, the Amalfi Coast offers a wide range of options for couples looking to celebrate their special moments. This detailed guide will provide an extensive and informative overview of honeymoon and anniversary ideas on the Amalfi Coast, ensuring that anyone planning a romantic getaway will have a comprehensive understanding of what the region has to offer.

One of the most important aspects of a honeymoon or anniversary trip is choosing the right accommodation. The Amalfi Coast is home to a variety of luxurious hotels and resorts that cater specifically to couples. One of the most renowned options is the Monastero Santa Rosa Hotel & Spa in Conca dei Marini. Perched on a cliff above the sea, this former monastery has been transformed into a luxurious retreat with stunning views of the coastline. The hotel offers elegant rooms and suites, a world-class spa, and a beautiful infinity pool that seems to blend seamlessly with the sea. The serene and exclusive atmosphere of the Monastero Santa Rosa makes it an ideal choice for couples seeking a romantic and intimate escape.

Another excellent accommodation option is the Belmond Hotel Caruso in Ravello. This historic hotel, set in a beautifully restored 11th-century building, offers a blend of old-world charm and modern luxury. The hotel features elegant rooms and suites, lush gardens, and an infinity pool with breathtaking views of the Amalfi Coast. The Belmond Hotel Caruso also offers a variety of romantic experiences, such as private dinners in the garden, couples' massages, and boat excursions along the coast. The combination of stunning scenery, luxurious amenities, and impeccable service makes the Belmond Hotel Caruso a perfect choice for a honeymoon or anniversary celebration.

For couples looking for a more contemporary and chic accommodation, Casa Angelina in Praiano offers a stylish and modern retreat. The hotel features minimalist design, bright and airy rooms, and stunning views of the sea. Casa Angelina's rooftop terrace is a highlight, offering a perfect spot for sunset cocktails and romantic dinners. The hotel's spa offers a range of treatments, including couples' massages and private wellness sessions. The relaxed and sophisticated atmosphere of Casa Angelina provides a perfect setting for a romantic and unforgettable stay.

Dining is another key element of a memorable honeymoon or anniversary trip, and the Amalfi Coast offers a wealth of fine dining options that cater to couples. One of the most celebrated restaurants in the region is Ristorante La Sponda in Positano. Located in the renowned Le Sirenuse Hotel, this restaurant is famous for its breathtaking views of the town and the sea, especially when illuminated at night. The restaurant's interior is equally enchanting, with candlelit tables and an abundance of greenery creating a magical ambiance. La Sponda offers a menu that highlights traditional Mediterranean flavors with a modern twist, using fresh, local ingredients. Dishes such as homemade pasta, fresh seafood, and decadent desserts are beautifully presented and paired with an extensive wine list. The impeccable service and stunning setting make La Sponda an unforgettable dining experience for couples.

Another top choice for a romantic dinner is Ristorante Eolo in Amalfi. Perched on a cliff overlooking the sea, Eolo provides a picturesque setting with panoramic views of the coastline. The restaurant features a charming terrace where couples can dine al fresco while enjoying the gentle sea breeze and the sound of the waves. Eolo's menu focuses on contemporary Italian cuisine with an emphasis on fresh seafood and locally sourced produce. Signature dishes include grilled octopus, lemon-infused risotto, and a variety of delectable desserts. The combination of exquisite food, attentive service, and a romantic setting makes Ristorante Eolo a perfect choice for a memorable dinner.

In Ravello, Ristorante Rossellinis at the Palazzo Avino offers an elegant and intimate dining experience. The restaurant's terrace provides stunning views of the Amalfi Coast, making it an ideal spot for a romantic evening. Rossellinis is known for its refined Italian cuisine, featuring dishes that showcase the best of local ingredients and culinary traditions. The menu includes a variety of appetizers, pasta dishes, and main courses, all expertly prepared and presented. Couples can enjoy a tasting menu that allows them to sample a range of flavors and textures, complemented by a carefully curated wine list. The sophisticated ambiance and exceptional cuisine make Rossellinis a top choice for a special night out.

For a truly unique and romantic dining experience, couples can visit Il Refettorio at the Monastero Santa Rosa Hotel & Spa. Housed in a former monastery, the restaurant offers a serene and historic setting with beautiful views of the sea. The dining room features vaulted ceilings and elegant decor, creating a sophisticated yet intimate atmosphere. Il Refettorio's menu is inspired by the flavors of the Amalfi Coast, with a focus on fresh, seasonal ingredients. Dishes such as handmade pasta, locally caught fish, and traditional desserts are crafted with care and creativity. The exceptional service and tranquil setting make Il Refettorio an ideal choice for a romantic dinner.

In addition to fine dining, the Amalfi Coast offers a variety of romantic activities and experiences that are perfect for couples celebrating a honeymoon or anniversary. One of the most popular activities is taking a private boat tour along the coast. These tours provide an intimate and personalized experience, with options ranging from half-day excursions to full-day adventures. Couples can explore hidden coves, secluded beaches, and picturesque villages, enjoying the stunning scenery and the sense of privacy. A sunset cruise is a particularly romantic option, offering the chance to watch the sun set over the Mediterranean Sea while sipping on a glass of Prosecco. Many tours also offer the option to visit the famous Blue Grotto on the island of Capri, a sea cave known for its stunning blue light.

For couples who enjoy exploring on foot, the Path of the Gods (Sentiero degli Dei) is a must-do experience. This famous hiking trail runs from the village of Bomerano in Agerola to Nocelle, a hamlet above Positano. The trail offers spectacular views of the coastline, the sea, and the surrounding mountains. Couples can take their time to explore the trail, enjoying the stunning scenery and the sense of tranquility. The Path of the Gods is well-marked and suitable for hikers of various levels, making it a popular choice for couples who enjoy outdoor activities. Along the way, hikers pass through terraced vineyards, ancient ruins, and charming villages, providing a diverse and enriching experience.

Exploring the picturesque towns of the Amalfi Coast is another romantic activity that couples can enjoy together. Positano, with its colorful buildings and narrow streets, is a favorite destination for couples. The town's main beach, Spiaggia Grande, provides a beautiful backdrop for relaxing by the sea, and the beachside bars and restaurants offer the perfect setting for a romantic meal with a view. Couples can also wander through the town's boutiques and art galleries, discovering unique souvenirs and local crafts. Another highlight is a visit to the Church of Santa Maria Assunta, which features a stunning Byzantine icon of the Black Madonna.

Amalfi, with its rich history and picturesque setting, is another top destination for couples. The town's charming streets, historic sites, and stunning views make it an ideal place for romantic exploration. A visit to the Amalfi Cathedral, with its striking facade and beautiful interior, provides a unique and intimate experience. Couples can also explore the town's many shops and cafes, enjoying the relaxed and welcoming atmosphere. A romantic walk along the seaside promenade, taking in the views of the harbor and the sea, is a must-do activity in Amalfi. The town's many restaurants, such as Ristorante Eolo, offer the perfect setting for a romantic dinner, with delicious cuisine and stunning views.

Ravello, perched high above the coast, is known for its breathtaking views and beautiful gardens, making it a perfect destination for couples. The town's main attractions, Villa Rufolo and Villa Cimbrone, offer some of the most romantic settings on the Amalfi Coast. The gardens of Villa Rufolo, with their exotic plants and stunning views, provide a peaceful and intimate setting for a romantic stroll. The Terrace of Infinity at Villa Cimbrone offers one of the most breathtaking views in Italy, with a sweeping panorama of the coastline and the sea. Couples can enjoy the serene atmosphere and the stunning scenery, creating unforgettable memories. Ravello is also known for its cultural events, such as the Ravello Festival, which features classical music concerts in the open-air gardens, providing a unique and romantic experience.

For a more secluded and intimate experience, the town of Atrani is a hidden gem on the Amalfi Coast. Located just a short distance from Amalfi, Atrani is one of the smallest and most picturesque towns in the region. Its narrow streets, archways, and small squares create a charming and intimate atmosphere, perfect for couples seeking a quiet and romantic escape. The town's main square, Piazza Umberto I, is a great place to relax and enjoy a coffee or gelato while watching the local life. Atrani's quiet and authentic charm makes it a hidden gem for couples looking to escape the more crowded tourist spots.

Maiori, with its long sandy beach and relaxed vibe, is another excellent destination for couples. The town offers a variety of activities, from lounging on the beach to exploring historical sites such as the Castle of San Nicola de Thoro-Plano, a medieval fortress with panoramic views. Couples can also visit the nearby Abbey of Santa Maria de Olearia, an ancient monastery with beautiful frescoes. Maiori's wide promenade is perfect for a leisurely stroll, and the town's numerous cafes and restaurants offer plenty of opportunities to sample local cuisine. The friendly and laid-back atmosphere of Maiori makes it an inviting destination for couples.

Minori, known as the "City of Taste," is a paradise for food lovers. The town is famous for its traditional pasta, particularly the hand-rolled "ndunderi," which is said to date back to Roman times. Couples can visit the local pasta shops and bakeries to sample these delicious treats. Minori is also home to the Villa Romana, an ancient Roman villa with well-preserved mosaics and frescoes. The town's lemon groves and terraced vineyards add to its charm, and couples can enjoy peaceful walks through the countryside. Minori's focus on food and tradition makes it a delightful destination for couples seeking a culinary adventure.

For couples who enjoy wine, a visit to a local vineyard is a must. The Amalfi Coast is home to several vineyards that produce excellent wines, particularly whites and rosés. Couples can take a guided tour of the vineyards, learning about the wine-making process and sampling a variety of wines. Many tours also include a visit to the cellar and a tasting of local products such as olive oil and cheese. One of the most renowned vineyards in the region is Marisa Cuomo, located in the town of Furore. The vineyard offers guided tours and tastings, providing couples with a unique and memorable experience.

Cooking classes are another excellent activity for couples on the Amalfi Coast. Many cooking schools and local chefs offer classes that teach participants how to prepare traditional dishes using fresh, local ingredients. These classes often include a visit to a local market to select ingredients, followed by a hands-on cooking session and a shared meal. Couples can enjoy the opportunity to learn new skills, meet other travelers, and savor the delicious results of their efforts. One notable option is Mamma Agata's Cooking School in Ravello, which offers a warm and welcoming environment and teaches participants to prepare a variety of traditional dishes.

Art and craft workshops provide another enriching activity for couples. The Amalfi Coast is known for its ceramics, paper-making, and textiles, and many local artisans offer workshops and classes where visitors can learn these traditional crafts. In Vietri sul Mare, couples can join a ceramics workshop to learn about the techniques and traditions of this craft and create their own hand-painted pieces. In Amalfi, the Paper Museum offers classes in traditional paper-making, allowing participants to create beautiful handmade paper using centuries-old methods. These workshops provide a unique and hands-on way to connect with the region's artistic heritage and create meaningful souvenirs.

Wellness and spa experiences are abundant on the Amalfi Coast, providing couples with the perfect opportunity to relax and rejuvenate together. Many hotels and wellness centers offer a range of treatments, from massages and facials to holistic therapies and yoga sessions. The Monastero Santa Rosa Hotel & Spa, perched on a cliff above the sea, offers a luxurious and serene retreat with a range of wellness treatments. Couples can enjoy the thermal suite, hydrotherapy pool, and a variety of spa treatments, all while taking in the stunning views of the coastline. The Caruso, A Belmond Hotel, in Ravello, also offers a world-class spa with indoor and outdoor treatment rooms, providing a perfect setting for relaxation and self-care.

The Amalfi Coast offers a wealth of activities and experiences that are perfect for couples celebrating a honeymoon or anniversary. From luxurious accommodations and fine dining to intimate experiences and adventurous activities, there are countless ways for couples to create unforgettable memories together. Each activity provides a unique and enriching experience, allowing couples to immerse themselves in the beauty, culture, and traditions of the Amalfi Coast. Whether you are seeking adventure, relaxation, or cultural enrichment, the Amalfi Coast provides the perfect backdrop for a romantic and memorable getaway.

CHAPTER 11

TRAVELING WITH KIDS

Family-Friendly Attractions

The Amalfi Coast is a beautiful and captivating destination, offering a wide range of family-friendly attractions that cater to all ages. From charming towns and historical sites to beautiful beaches and scenic hikes, the region provides endless opportunities for families to create unforgettable memories together.

One of the most popular family-friendly destinations on the Amalfi Coast is the town of Amalfi. With its rich history, picturesque setting, and numerous attractions, Amalfi is a must-visit for families. The town's main square, Piazza Duomo, is home to the stunning Amalfi Cathedral. The cathedral's striking facade and beautiful interior are sure to captivate both adults and children. Families can explore the cathedral's crypt, cloister, and museum, learning about the town's history and its significance as a maritime republic. The Paper Museum (Museo della Carta) in Amalfi is another excellent attraction for families. Housed in a historic paper mill, the museum offers guided tours and demonstrations of traditional paper-making techniques. Children will enjoy seeing the machinery in action and creating their own handmade paper.

For a fun and educational experience, families can visit the Valle delle Ferriere, a nature reserve located near Amalfi. The reserve offers several hiking trails that take visitors through lush forests, past waterfalls, and along ancient aqueducts. The trails are well-marked and suitable for families with children of all ages. The Valle delle Ferriere is home to a variety of plant and animal species, and families can learn about the local flora and fauna while enjoying the natural beauty of the area. The reserve also includes the remains of ancient ironworks, adding a historical dimension to the hike.

Positano is another top destination for families on the Amalfi Coast. Known for its colorful buildings and beautiful beaches, Positano offers a range of family-friendly activities. The town's main beach, Spiaggia Grande, is a great place for families to relax and enjoy the sun and sea. The beach is equipped with facilities such as sun loungers, umbrellas, and beachside cafes, making it easy for families to spend a day by the water. For a more active experience, families can rent paddleboats or kayaks and explore the coastline from the sea. Positano also offers several boat tours that take visitors to nearby attractions such as the Li Galli islands and the Blue Grotto on Capri. These tours provide a fun and exciting way for families to see the region's natural beauty and marine life.

Ravello, perched high above the coast, is known for its breathtaking views and beautiful gardens, making it a perfect destination for families. The town's main attractions, Villa

Rufolo and Villa Cimbrone, offer some of the most stunning settings on the Amalfi Coast. The gardens of Villa Rufolo, with their exotic plants and panoramic views, provide a peaceful and enchanting place for families to explore. Children will enjoy wandering through the gardens, discovering hidden paths and secret corners. The Terrace of Infinity at Villa Cimbrone offers one of the most breathtaking views in Italy, with a sweeping panorama of the coastline and the sea. Families can enjoy the serene atmosphere and the stunning scenery, creating unforgettable memories together.

Maiori, with its long sandy beach and relaxed vibe, is another excellent destination for families. The town offers a variety of activities, from lounging on the beach to exploring historical sites such as the Castle of San Nicola de Thoro-Plano, a medieval fortress with panoramic views. Families can also visit the nearby Abbey of Santa Maria de Olearia, an ancient monastery with beautiful frescoes. Maiori's wide promenade is perfect for a leisurely stroll, and the town's numerous cafes and restaurants offer plenty of opportunities to sample local cuisine. The friendly and laid-back atmosphere of Maiori makes it an inviting destination for families.

Minori, known as the "City of Taste," is a paradise for food lovers and a great destination for families. The town is famous for its traditional pasta, particularly the hand-rolled "ndunderi," which is said to date back to Roman times.

Families can visit the local pasta shops and bakeries to sample these delicious treats. Minori is also home to the Villa Romana, an ancient Roman villa with well-preserved mosaics and frescoes. The town's lemon groves and terraced vineyards add to its charm, and families can enjoy peaceful walks through the countryside. Minori's focus on food and tradition makes it a delightful destination for families seeking a culinary adventure.

For families interested in marine life, a visit to the Marine Protected Area of Punta Campanella is a must. Located near the town of Massa Lubrense, this protected area offers snorkeling and diving opportunities that allow visitors to explore the underwater world of the Amalfi Coast. Families can see a variety of marine species, including colorful fish, sea urchins, and octopuses. The area is also home to several ancient shipwrecks, adding an element of adventure and discovery to the experience. Guided snorkeling and diving tours are available, providing equipment and instruction for families with children.

The island of Capri, located just off the coast, is another top destination for families. Known for its rugged landscape, upscale shops, and stunning views, Capri offers a variety of experiences for families. One of the highlights of a visit to Capri is a boat tour around the island, which includes a visit to the famous Blue Grotto, a sea cave with mesmerizing blue waters. Families can also take the chairlift to Monte Solaro, the highest point on the island, for panoramic views of the coastline and the sea. The town of Anacapri offers a more laid-back atmosphere and several family-friendly attractions, including the Villa San Michele, a historic villa with beautiful gardens and a small museum.

For a unique and educational experience, families can visit the archaeological site of Pompeii, located just a short distance from the Amalfi Coast. The well-preserved ruins of this ancient Roman city offer a fascinating glimpse into daily life in the first century AD. Families can explore the streets of Pompeii, visiting houses, temples, and public buildings, and learn about the catastrophic eruption of Mount Vesuvius that buried the city. Guided tours are available and provide valuable context and information, making the visit more engaging and informative for children.

In addition to these specific attractions, the Amalfi Coast offers a variety of family-friendly activities and experiences. Many towns along the coast have local markets where families can shop for fresh produce, handmade crafts, and local specialties. These markets provide a fun and interactive way for children to experience the local culture and cuisine. Cooking classes are another excellent activity for families, allowing children to learn about traditional Italian dishes and participate in the cooking process. Many cooking schools and local chefs offer classes specifically designed for families, making it a fun and educational experience for all ages.

Boat rentals and sailing excursions are also popular family activities on the Amalfi Coast. Families can rent a small boat or join a guided sailing tour to explore the coastline, visit hidden beaches, and swim in the clear blue waters of the Mediterranean Sea. These excursions provide a unique perspective on the region's natural beauty and offer plenty of opportunities for family fun and adventure.

Finally, the Amalfi Coast is home to several festivals and events that are enjoyable for families. The Ravello Festival, held each summer, features classical music concerts and cultural events in the town's beautiful gardens and historic sites. The Festival of San Gennaro in Praiano is another family-friendly event, with processions, fireworks, and traditional music and dance. These festivals provide a lively and festive atmosphere, allowing families to experience the local culture and traditions.

The Amalfi Coast offers a wealth of family-friendly attractions and activities that cater to all ages and interests. From exploring historical sites and beautiful gardens to enjoying the beaches and participating in hands-on activities, there are countless ways for families to create unforgettable memories together. Each attraction provides a unique and enriching experience, allowing families to immerse themselves in the beauty, culture, and traditions of the Amalfi Coast. Whether you are seeking adventure, relaxation, or cultural enrichment, the Amalfi Coast provides the perfect backdrop for a family-friendly and memorable getaway.

Kid-Friendly Restaurants

The Amalfi Coast, renowned for its breathtaking landscapes, historical richness, and vibrant culture, is also a wonderful destination for families traveling with children. One of the most delightful aspects of visiting this beautiful region is the opportunity to enjoy its delicious cuisine in a variety of settings. Finding kid-friendly restaurants that cater to the tastes and needs of younger guests is important for ensuring a pleasant dining experience for the whole family.

One of the top kid-friendly restaurants in Positano is Chez Black, located right on the beach. This well-loved restaurant has been serving delicious Italian cuisine since 1949 and offers a warm, welcoming atmosphere that is perfect for families. The menu features a wide variety of dishes, including pizza, pasta, and fresh seafood, ensuring there is something for everyone. Kids will particularly enjoy the wood-fired pizzas and homemade pasta dishes. The restaurant's lively and friendly staff are great with children, making dining here a fun and relaxed experience. The seaside location also means families can enjoy beautiful views while they eat.

Another great option in Positano is Ristorante La Cambusa. This restaurant, also located near the beach, offers a diverse menu that includes a range of kid-friendly options. The spacious outdoor seating area is ideal for families, providing plenty of room for children to move around. The menu includes favorites such as spaghetti, pizza, and grilled fish, all made with fresh, local ingredients. La Cambusa's relaxed atmosphere and attentive service make it a popular choice for families looking to enjoy a meal together in a picturesque setting.

In the town of Amalfi, Pizzeria Donna Stella is a fantastic choice for families. This charming pizzeria is known for its delicious, wood-fired pizzas, which are sure to be a hit with kids. The restaurant features a beautiful outdoor garden seating area, providing a relaxed and enjoyable environment for dining. The menu includes a variety of pizza toppings, allowing children to choose their favorites. In addition to pizza, Donna Stella also offers a selection of salads and appetizers, making it a great option for a casual family meal.

For a more traditional Italian dining experience, families can visit Trattoria da Gemma in Amalfi. This restaurant has been serving classic Italian dishes for over 80 years and offers a warm, family-friendly atmosphere. The menu includes a variety of pasta dishes, risottos, and meat entrees, with many options that are sure to appeal to children. The restaurant's central location and welcoming staff make it a convenient and enjoyable choice for families exploring the town.

Maiori, known for its long sandy beach, is home to several kid-friendly restaurants. One standout option is Torre Normanna, a restaurant housed in a historic Norman tower. The unique setting and stunning views of the sea make dining here a special experience for families. The menu features a range of Italian dishes, including seafood, pasta, and pizza, ensuring there is something for everyone. The restaurant also offers a children's menu with smaller portions and kid-friendly options. The combination of delicious food, attentive service, and a beautiful location make Torre Normanna a great choice for families visiting Maiori.

Another excellent restaurant in Maiori is Ristorante Pineta 1903. This family-run establishment offers a warm and inviting atmosphere, with a menu that includes a variety of kid-friendly dishes. The restaurant features a spacious garden seating area, providing plenty of room for children to play while waiting for their meal. The menu includes classic Italian dishes such as pasta, pizza, and grilled meats, all made with fresh, local ingredients. The friendly staff and relaxed environment make Ristorante Pineta 1903 a popular choice for families.

In the town of Minori, Pasticceria Sal De Riso is a must-visit for families with a sweet tooth. This famous pastry shop, owned by renowned pastry chef Salvatore De Riso, offers a wide variety of delicious desserts, including cakes, pastries, and gelato. The shop also features a small café where families can enjoy a light meal or snack. Kids will love the colorful and tasty treats, while parents can relax with a cup of coffee or a glass of wine. The central location and delightful offerings make Pasticceria Sal De Riso a favorite stop for families visiting Minori.

For a more casual dining experience, families can visit A Ricetta in Minori. This restaurant offers a relaxed and welcoming atmosphere, with a menu that includes a variety of Italian dishes. The spacious outdoor seating area is perfect for families, providing plenty of room for children to move around. The menu includes kid-friendly options such as pizza, pasta, and grilled chicken, all made with fresh ingredients. The friendly staff and casual environment make A Ricetta a great choice for a family meal.

In the town of Praiano, Il Pirata is a fantastic option for families. This seaside restaurant offers stunning views of the sea and a relaxed, family-friendly atmosphere. The menu features a variety of Italian dishes, including seafood, pasta, and pizza, ensuring there is something for everyone. The restaurant also offers a children's menu with smaller portions and kid-friendly options. The combination of delicious food, attentive service, and a beautiful location make Il Pirata a great choice for families visiting Praiano.

Another excellent restaurant in Praiano is La Moressa. This family-friendly establishment offers a warm and inviting atmosphere, with a menu that includes a variety of Italian dishes. The restaurant features a spacious outdoor seating area, providing plenty of room for children to play while waiting for their meal. The menu includes classic Italian dishes such as pasta, pizza, and grilled meats, all made with fresh, local ingredients. The friendly staff and relaxed environment make La Moressa a popular choice for families.

For families visiting the island of Capri, Ristorante Verginiello is a top choice. This restaurant offers stunning views of the sea and a relaxed, family-friendly atmosphere. The menu features a variety of Italian dishes, including seafood, pasta, and pizza, ensuring there is something for everyone. The restaurant also offers a children's menu with smaller portions and kid-friendly options. The combination of delicious food, attentive service, and a beautiful location make Ristorante Verginiello a great choice for families visiting Capri.

Another excellent restaurant on Capri is Ristorante da Paolino. Known for its beautiful lemon grove setting, this restaurant offers a unique and memorable dining experience for families. The menu features a variety of Italian dishes, including seafood, pasta, and pizza, all made with fresh, local ingredients. Kids will love the outdoor setting and the friendly atmosphere, while parents can relax and enjoy the delicious food. The combination of beautiful surroundings, delicious cuisine, and a family-friendly atmosphere make Ristorante da Paolino a great choice for a family meal.

The Amalfi Coast offers a wide range of kid-friendly restaurants that cater to families traveling with children. From casual pizzerias and pastry shops to fine dining establishments with stunning views, there is something to suit every taste and preference. Each restaurant provides a unique and enjoyable dining experience, allowing families to savor the delicious cuisine of the region while ensuring that children are happy and entertained. By exploring these top kid-friendly restaurants, families can create unforgettable memories and enjoy the best of what the Amalfi Coast has to offer. Whether you are seeking a casual meal by the beach or a special dining experience in a historic setting, the Amalfi Coast provides the perfect backdrop for a memorable family meal.

Activities for Children

The Amalfi Coast, with its stunning landscapes, charming towns, and rich cultural heritage, is a fantastic destination for families with children. There are numerous activities that cater to young travelers, ensuring that they remain entertained and engaged throughout their visit.

One of the most enjoyable activities for children on the Amalfi Coast is spending time at the beach. The coast is dotted with beautiful beaches that are perfect for families. Spiaggia Grande in Positano is one of the most popular beaches and offers plenty of space for children to play and swim. The beach is equipped with facilities such as sun loungers, umbrellas, and beachside cafes, making it easy for families to spend a whole day by the sea. Children can build sandcastles, paddle in the shallow waters, and enjoy the lively atmosphere.

For a more secluded beach experience, families can visit Marina di Praia in Praiano. This small, pebbly beach is nestled between cliffs and offers a peaceful and safe environment for children. The calm waters are ideal for swimming and snorkeling, and the beach is less crowded than some of the larger ones on the coast. There are also a few restaurants nearby where families can enjoy a meal with a view of the sea.

Another fantastic activity for children is taking a boat tour along the Amalfi Coast. These tours provide a fun and exciting way to see the coastline and explore hidden coves and beaches that are only accessible by boat. Many boat tours offer the opportunity to swim and snorkel in the clear blue waters, which is sure to be a highlight for kids. A visit to the famous Blue Grotto on the island of Capri is a must-do. The grotto's stunning blue light and the adventure of entering the cave by boat will captivate children and create lasting memories.

Exploring the towns of the Amalfi Coast can also be a delightful experience for children. Positano, with its colorful buildings and narrow streets, is particularly enchanting. Children will enjoy wandering through the town, discovering its many shops and cafes. A visit to the Church of Santa Maria Assunta, with its beautiful Byzantine icon of the Black Madonna, offers a glimpse into the town's rich history. Another highlight is the Positano Art Walk, which features a series of art installations and sculptures along the town's streets, providing a fun and educational experience for children.

In Amalfi, the Paper Museum (Museo della Carta) is a great place to visit with children. Housed in a historic paper mill, the museum offers guided tours and demonstrations of traditional paper-making techniques. Children will enjoy seeing the machinery in action and creating their own handmade paper. The museum also provides an educational experience, teaching visitors about the history of paper-making in Amalfi and its importance to the town's economy.

Ravello, known for its breathtaking views and beautiful gardens, is another top destination for families. The town's main attractions, Villa Rufolo and Villa Cimbrone, offer some of the most stunning settings on the Amalfi Coast. The gardens of Villa Rufolo, with their exotic plants and panoramic views, provide a peaceful and enchanting place for children to explore. The Terrace of Infinity at Villa Cimbrone offers one of the most breathtaking views in Italy, with a sweeping panorama of the coastline and the sea. Children will enjoy the adventure of exploring these beautiful gardens and discovering hidden paths and secret corners.

For families interested in hiking, the Path of the Gods (Sentiero degli Dei) is a must-do experience. This famous hiking trail runs from the village of Bomerano in Agerola to Nocelle, a hamlet above Positano. The trail offers spectacular views of the coastline, the sea, and the surrounding mountains. While the hike can be challenging, it is suitable for older children and teenagers who enjoy outdoor activities. The Path of the Gods is well-marked and provides a sense of adventure and accomplishment for young hikers. Along the way, hikers pass through terraced vineyards, ancient ruins, and charming villages, providing a diverse and enriching experience.

Another excellent activity for children is visiting the Valle delle Ferriere, a nature reserve located near Amalfi. The reserve offers several hiking trails that take visitors through lush forests, past waterfalls, and along ancient aqueducts. The trails are well-marked and suitable for families with children of all ages. The Valle delle Ferriere is home to a variety of plant and animal species, and children can learn about the local flora and fauna while enjoying the natural beauty of the area. The reserve also includes the remains of ancient ironworks, adding a historical dimension to the hike.

For a more educational experience, families can visit the archaeological site of Pompeii, located just a short distance from the Amalfi Coast. The well-preserved ruins of this ancient Roman city offer a fascinating glimpse into daily life in the first century AD. Children will enjoy exploring the streets of Pompeii, visiting houses, temples, and public buildings, and learning about the catastrophic eruption of Mount Vesuvius that buried the city. Guided tours are available and provide valuable context and information, making the visit more engaging and informative for children.

Cooking classes are another excellent activity for families on the Amalfi Coast. Many cooking schools and local chefs offer classes that teach participants how to prepare traditional dishes using fresh, local ingredients. These classes often include a visit to a local market to select ingredients, followed by a hands-on cooking session and a shared meal. Children will enjoy the opportunity to learn new skills and participate in the cooking process. One notable option is Mamma Agata's Cooking School in Ravello, which offers a warm and welcoming environment and teaches participants to prepare a variety of traditional dishes.

For families visiting the island of Capri, the chairlift to Monte Solaro is a fun and exciting activity. The chairlift takes visitors to the highest point on the island, offering panoramic views of the coastline and the sea. Children will enjoy the adventure of riding the chairlift and the stunning views from the top. The town of Anacapri, located nearby, offers a more laid-back atmosphere and several family-friendly attractions, including the Villa San Michele, a historic villa with beautiful gardens and a small museum.

For a unique and educational experience, families can visit the Marine Protected Area of Punta Campanella, located near the town of Massa Lubrense. This protected area offers snorkeling and diving opportunities that allow visitors to explore the underwater world of the Amalfi Coast. Children can see a variety of marine species, including colorful fish, sea urchins, and octopuses. The area is also home to several ancient shipwrecks, adding an element of adventure and discovery to the experience. Guided snorkeling and diving tours are available, providing equipment and instruction for families with children.

The Amalfi Coast offers a wide range of activities for children that cater to all ages and interests. From spending time at the beach and exploring charming towns to hiking scenic trails and participating in hands-on activities, there are countless ways for families to create unforgettable memories together. Each activity provides a unique and enriching experience, allowing children to immerse themselves in the beauty, culture, and traditions of the Amalfi Coast. Whether you are seeking adventure, relaxation, or educational enrichment, the Amalfi Coast provides the perfect backdrop for a family-friendly and memorable getaway.

Tips for Traveling with Young Kids

Traveling with young kids to the Amalfi Coast can be a delightful and enriching experience, but it requires careful planning and consideration to ensure that the trip is enjoyable and stress-free for the entire family. The Amalfi Coast, with its stunning scenery, charming towns, and rich cultural heritage, offers numerous opportunities for family fun and bonding. This detailed guide provides extensive and informative tips for traveling with young kids on the Amalfi Coast, ensuring that anyone planning a family trip will have a comprehensive understanding of how to make the most of their visit.

One of the first things to consider when traveling with young kids is accommodation. Choosing family-friendly accommodation is crucial to ensure a comfortable stay. Many hotels and resorts on the Amalfi Coast cater specifically to families, offering amenities such as cribs, high chairs, and family rooms. When booking accommodation, it's a good idea to check for these amenities and to confirm that the hotel can accommodate your family's specific needs. Staying in a central location, such as Amalfi, Positano, or Maiori, can also be convenient as it reduces travel time to key attractions and provides easy access to restaurants, shops, and medical facilities.

Packing appropriately for a trip with young kids is essential. In addition to the usual clothing and toiletries, it's important to bring items that will keep children comfortable and entertained during the trip. This includes favorite snacks, toys, books, and electronic devices with headphones. A good stroller is also a must-have, especially for exploring the narrow and often steep streets of the Amalfi Coast towns. A lightweight, foldable stroller is ideal as it can be easily transported and stored. It's also useful to bring a baby carrier for younger children, particularly when visiting places that may not be stroller-friendly.

Traveling by car can be one of the most convenient ways to explore the Amalfi Coast with young kids, as it allows for flexibility and ease of transport. Renting a car with adequate space for car seats and luggage is important. Make sure to bring or rent car seats that meet safety standards, as these are required by law in Italy for young children. Be prepared for the winding and narrow roads of the Amalfi Coast, which can be challenging to navigate, but also offer some of the most breathtaking views.

Public transportation, including buses and ferries, is another option for getting around the Amalfi Coast. The SITA bus service connects the main towns along the coast and is an affordable way to travel. However, buses can get crowded, especially during peak tourist season, so it's advisable to travel during off-peak hours when possible. Ferries offer a scenic and enjoyable way to travel between coastal towns and are often less crowded than buses. Kids will love the experience of traveling by boat, and the views from the water are spectacular.

Meal times can be a highlight of the trip, but it's important to choose kid-friendly restaurants that offer a variety of options to suit young palates. Many restaurants on the Amalfi Coast are family-friendly and offer high chairs and children's menus. Italian cuisine is generally well-loved by kids, with dishes like pizza, pasta, and gelato being sure favorites. It's a good idea to familiarize yourself with the restaurant options in the area and make reservations in advance, especially for popular dining spots. Packing some snacks and drinks for the day can also be helpful, particularly when exploring or traveling between towns.

Ensuring the safety of young kids while exploring the Amalfi Coast is paramount. Many of the towns are built on steep cliffs, with narrow streets and steps. It's important to keep a close eye on children and hold their hands, especially in busy areas or near steep drop-offs. Wearing comfortable and sturdy footwear is essential for both adults and children, as the terrain can be uneven. Sunscreen, hats, and sunglasses are also important to protect against the strong Mediterranean sun.

Keeping young kids entertained during the trip can make a significant difference in the overall experience. The Amalfi Coast offers a variety of activities that are enjoyable for children. Beach days are always a hit, and there are several family-friendly beaches along the coast. Spiaggia Grande in Positano and the beach in Maiori are both excellent options, offering facilities such as sun loungers, umbrellas, and beachside cafes. Kids can play in the sand, paddle in the shallow waters, and enjoy the lively atmosphere.

Exploring the towns of the Amalfi Coast can be an adventure for young kids. Positano, with its colorful buildings and narrow streets, is particularly enchanting. Children will enjoy wandering through the town, discovering its many shops and cafes. A visit to the Church of Santa Maria Assunta, with its beautiful Byzantine icon of the Black Madonna, offers a glimpse into the town's rich history. Amalfi's Paper Museum (Museo della Carta) is another excellent attraction for families. Housed in a historic paper mill, the museum offers guided tours and demonstrations of traditional paper-making techniques. Children will enjoy seeing the machinery in action and creating their own handmade paper.

For a more active experience, families can visit the Valle delle Ferriere, a nature reserve located near Amalfi. The reserve offers several hiking trails that take visitors through lush forests, past waterfalls, and along ancient aqueducts. The trails are well-marked and suitable for families with children of all ages. The Valle delle Ferriere is home to a variety of plant and animal species, and children can learn about the local flora and fauna while enjoying the natural beauty of the area. The reserve also includes the remains of ancient ironworks, adding a historical dimension to the hike.

A visit to the island of Capri can be a highlight of a trip to the Amalfi Coast. The island offers several family-friendly attractions, including the chairlift to Monte Solaro, the highest point on the island. The chairlift provides stunning views of the coastline and the sea, and children will enjoy the adventure of riding to the top. The town of Anacapri, located nearby, offers a more laid-back atmosphere and several family-friendly attractions, including the Villa San Michele, a historic villa with beautiful gardens and a small museum.

Cooking classes are another excellent activity for families on the Amalfi Coast. Many cooking schools and local chefs offer classes that teach participants how to prepare traditional dishes using fresh, local ingredients. These classes often include a visit to a local market to select ingredients, followed by a hands-on cooking session and a shared meal. Children will enjoy the opportunity to learn new skills and participate in the cooking process. One notable option is Mamma Agata's Cooking School in Ravello, which offers a warm and welcoming environment and teaches participants to prepare a variety of traditional dishes.

For a unique and educational experience, families can visit the archaeological site of Pompeii, located just a short distance from the Amalfi Coast. The well-preserved ruins of this ancient Roman city offer a fascinating glimpse into daily life in the first century AD. Children will enjoy exploring the streets of Pompeii, visiting houses, temples, and public buildings, and learning about the catastrophic eruption of Mount Vesuvius that buried the city. Guided tours are available and provide valuable context and information, making the visit more engaging and informative for children.

Traveling with young kids to the Amalfi Coast can be a rewarding and enjoyable experience with the right preparation and planning. By choosing family-friendly accommodation, packing appropriately, and planning activities that cater to children's interests and needs, families can create unforgettable memories together. The Amalfi Coast offers a wealth of experiences, from relaxing beach days and scenic boat tours to exploring charming towns and participating in hands-on activities. Each experience provides a unique and enriching opportunity for children to immerse themselves in the beauty, culture, and traditions of the Amalfi Coast. Whether you are seeking adventure, relaxation, or educational enrichment, the Amalfi Coast provides the perfect backdrop for a family-friendly and memorable getaway.

CHAPTER 12

TRAVELING AS A FAMILY

Top Family Destinations

The Amalfi Coast is an exceptional destination for families, offering a blend of natural beauty, historical sites, and cultural experiences that can be enjoyed by all ages. With its stunning coastline, charming towns, and a wealth of activities, the Amalfi Coast is a perfect place for families to create lasting memories together.

One of the most family-friendly destinations on the Amalfi Coast is Positano. This picturesque town, with its colorful buildings cascading down the cliffs to the sea, offers a variety of activities that can be enjoyed by families. The main beach, Spiaggia Grande, is a favorite spot for families, providing plenty of space for children to play and swim. The beach is equipped with sun loungers, umbrellas, and beachside cafes, making it easy for families to spend a relaxing day by the sea. The shallow waters are safe for young swimmers, and the beach is often less crowded in the early morning and late afternoon, providing a more peaceful experience.

Positano's narrow streets and charming shops are perfect for leisurely strolls. Families can explore the town, stopping to enjoy gelato or browse the local boutiques. The Church of Santa Maria Assunta, with its beautiful Byzantine icon of the

Black Madonna, is a must-see attraction. Children will be fascinated by the church's history and the colorful majolica-tiled dome. Positano also offers several family-friendly restaurants that serve delicious Italian cuisine, ensuring that even the pickiest eaters will find something to enjoy.

Another top family destination is Amalfi, known for its rich history and stunning setting. The town's main square, Piazza Duomo, is home to the impressive Amalfi Cathedral. Families can explore the cathedral's crypt, cloister, and museum, learning about the town's history and its significance as a maritime republic. The Paper Museum (Museo della Carta) in Amalfi is another excellent attraction for families. Housed in a historic paper mill, the museum offers guided tours and demonstrations of traditional paper-making techniques. Children will enjoy seeing the machinery in action and creating their own handmade paper.

For a fun and educational experience, families can visit the Valle delle Ferriere, a nature reserve located near Amalfi. The reserve offers several hiking trails that take visitors through lush forests, past waterfalls, and along ancient aqueducts. The trails are well-marked and suitable for families with children of all ages. The Valle delle Ferriere is home to a variety of plant and animal species, and families can learn about the local flora and fauna while enjoying the natural beauty of the area. The reserve also includes the remains of ancient ironworks, adding a historical dimension to the hike.

Ravello, perched high above the coast, is another top destination for families. The town's main attractions, Villa Rufolo and Villa Cimbrone, offer some of the most stunning settings on the Amalfi Coast. The gardens of Villa Rufolo, with their exotic plants and panoramic views, provide a peaceful and enchanting place for families to explore. Children will enjoy wandering through the gardens, discovering hidden paths and secret corners. The Terrace of Infinity at Villa Cimbrone offers one of the most breathtaking views in Italy, with a sweeping panorama of the coastline and the sea. Families can enjoy the serene atmosphere and the stunning scenery, creating unforgettable memories together.

Maiori, with its long sandy beach and relaxed vibe, is another excellent destination for families. The town offers a variety of activities, from lounging on the beach to exploring historical sites such as the Castle of San Nicola de Thoro-Plano, a medieval fortress with panoramic views. Families can also visit the nearby Abbey of Santa Maria de Olearia, an ancient monastery with beautiful frescoes. Maiori's wide promenade is perfect for a leisurely stroll, and the town's numerous cafes and restaurants offer plenty of opportunities to sample local cuisine. The friendly and laid-back atmosphere of Maiori makes it an inviting destination for families.

Minori, known as the "City of Taste," is a paradise for food lovers and a great destination for families. The town is famous for its traditional pasta, particularly the hand-rolled "ndunderi," which is said to date back to Roman times. Families can visit the local pasta shops and bakeries to sample these delicious treats. Minori is also home to the Villa Romana, an ancient Roman villa with well-preserved mosaics and frescoes. The town's lemon groves and terraced vineyards add to its charm, and families can enjoy peaceful walks through the countryside. Minori's focus on food and tradition makes it a delightful destination for families seeking a culinary adventure.

For families interested in marine life, a visit to the Marine Protected Area of Punta Campanella is a must. Located near the town of Massa Lubrense, this protected area offers snorkeling and diving opportunities that allow visitors to explore the underwater world of the Amalfi Coast. Families can see a variety of marine species, including colorful fish, sea urchins, and octopuses. The area is also home to several ancient shipwrecks, adding an element of adventure and discovery to the experience. Guided snorkeling and diving tours are available, providing equipment and instruction for families with children.

The island of Capri, located just off the coast, is another top destination for families. Known for its rugged landscape, upscale shops, and stunning views, Capri offers a variety of experiences for families. One of the highlights of a visit to

Capri is a boat tour around the island, which includes a visit to the famous Blue Grotto, a sea cave with mesmerizing blue waters. Families can also take the chairlift to Monte Solaro, the highest point on the island, for panoramic views of the coastline and the sea. The town of Anacapri offers a more laid-back atmosphere and several family-friendly attractions, including the Villa San Michele, a historic villa with beautiful gardens and a small museum.

For a unique and educational experience, families can visit the archaeological site of Pompeii, located just a short distance from the Amalfi Coast. The well-preserved ruins of this ancient Roman city offer a fascinating glimpse into daily life in the first century AD. Families can explore the streets of Pompeii, visiting houses, temples, and public buildings, and learn about the catastrophic eruption of Mount Vesuvius that buried the city. Guided tours are available and provide valuable context and information, making the visit more engaging and informative for children.

Cooking classes are another excellent activity for families on the Amalfi Coast. Many cooking schools and local chefs offer classes that teach participants how to prepare traditional dishes using fresh, local ingredients. These classes often include a visit to a local market to select ingredients, followed by a hands-on cooking session and a shared meal. Children will enjoy the opportunity to learn new skills and participate in the cooking process. One notable option is Mamma Agata's Cooking School in

Ravello, which offers a warm and welcoming environment and teaches participants to prepare a variety of traditional dishes.

Boat rentals and sailing excursions are also popular family activities on the Amalfi Coast. Families can rent a small boat or join a guided sailing tour to explore the coastline, visit hidden beaches, and swim in the clear blue waters of the Mediterranean Sea. These excursions provide a unique perspective on the region's natural beauty and offer plenty of opportunities for family fun and adventure.

The Amalfi Coast is also home to several festivals and events that are enjoyable for families. The Ravello Festival, held each summer, features classical music concerts and cultural events in the town's beautiful gardens and historic sites. The Festival of San Gennaro in Praiano is another family-friendly event, with processions, fireworks, and traditional music and dance. These festivals provide a lively and festive atmosphere, allowing families to experience the local culture and traditions.

In addition to these specific attractions, the Amalfi Coast offers a variety of family-friendly activities and experiences. Many towns along the coast have local markets where families can shop for fresh produce, handmade crafts, and local specialties. These markets provide a fun and interactive way for children to experience the local culture and cuisine.

The vibrant atmosphere and the variety of goods on offer make these markets a delightful experience for families.

Each destination provides a unique and enriching experience, allowing families to immerse themselves in the beauty, culture, and traditions of the Amalfi Coast. Whether you are seeking adventure, relaxation, or cultural enrichment, the Amalfi Coast provides the perfect backdrop for a family-friendly and memorable getaway.

Family Activities and Tours

The Amalfi Coast is a stunning destination that offers a wealth of activities and tours for families, providing endless opportunities for fun, adventure, and bonding. With its breathtaking landscapes, rich history, and vibrant culture, the Amalfi Coast is an ideal place for families to explore together.

One of the most enjoyable activities for families on the Amalfi Coast is spending time at the beach. The coastline is dotted with beautiful beaches that are perfect for families. Spiaggia Grande in Positano is one of the most popular beaches and offers plenty of space for children to play and swim. The beach is equipped with facilities such as sun loungers, umbrellas, and beachside cafes, making it easy for families to spend a relaxing day by the sea. The shallow waters are safe for young swimmers, and the beach is often less crowded in the early morning and late afternoon, providing a more peaceful experience.

For a more secluded beach experience, families can visit Marina di Praia in Praiano. This small, pebbly beach is nestled between cliffs and offers a peaceful and safe environment for children. The calm waters are ideal for swimming and snorkeling, and the beach is less crowded than some of the larger ones on the coast. There are also a few restaurants nearby where families can enjoy a meal with a view of the sea.

Another fantastic activity for families is taking a boat tour along the Amalfi Coast. These tours provide a fun and exciting way to see the coastline and explore hidden coves and beaches that are only accessible by boat. Many boat tours offer the opportunity to swim and snorkel in the clear blue waters, which is sure to be a highlight for kids. A visit to the famous Blue Grotto on the island of Capri is a must-do. The grotto's stunning blue light and the adventure of entering the cave by boat will captivate children and create lasting memories.

Exploring the towns of the Amalfi Coast can also be a delightful experience for families. Positano, with its colorful buildings and narrow streets, is particularly enchanting. Children will enjoy wandering through the town, discovering its many shops and cafes. A visit to the Church of Santa Maria Assunta, with its beautiful Byzantine icon of the Black Madonna, offers a glimpse into the town's rich history. Another highlight is the Positano Art Walk, which features a series of art installations and sculptures along the town's streets, providing a fun and educational experience for children.

In Amalfi, the Paper Museum (Museo della Carta) is a great place to visit with children. Housed in a historic paper mill, the museum offers guided tours and demonstrations of traditional paper-making techniques. Children will enjoy seeing the machinery in action and creating their own handmade paper. The museum also provides an educational experience, teaching visitors about the history of paper-making in Amalfi and its importance to the town's economy.

For a more active experience, families can visit the Valle delle Ferriere, a nature reserve located near Amalfi. The reserve offers several hiking trails that take visitors through lush forests, past waterfalls, and along ancient aqueducts. The trails are well-marked and suitable for families with children of all ages. The Valle delle Ferriere is home to a variety of plant and animal species, and families can learn about the local flora and fauna while enjoying the natural beauty of the area. The reserve also includes the remains of ancient ironworks, adding a historical dimension to the hike.

Ravello, perched high above the coast, is another top destination for families. The town's main attractions, Villa Rufolo and Villa Cimbrone, offer some of the most stunning settings on the Amalfi Coast. The gardens of Villa Rufolo, with their exotic plants and panoramic views, provide a peaceful and enchanting place for families to explore.

Children will enjoy wandering through the gardens, discovering hidden paths and secret corners. The Terrace of Infinity at Villa Cimbrone offers one of the most breathtaking views in Italy, with a sweeping panorama of the coastline and the sea. Families can enjoy the serene atmosphere and the stunning scenery, creating unforgettable memories together.

For a more educational experience, families can visit the archaeological site of Pompeii, located just a short distance from the Amalfi Coast. The well-preserved ruins of this ancient Roman city offer a fascinating glimpse into daily life in the first century AD. Families can explore the streets of Pompeii, visiting houses, temples, and public buildings, and learn about the catastrophic eruption of Mount Vesuvius that buried the city. Guided tours are available and provide valuable context and information, making the visit more engaging and informative for children.

Another exciting activity for families is visiting the island of Capri. The island offers several family-friendly attractions, including the chairlift to Monte Solaro, the highest point on the island. The chairlift provides stunning views of the coastline and the sea, and children will enjoy the adventure of riding to the top. The town of Anacapri, located nearby, offers a more laid-back atmosphere and several family-friendly attractions, including the Villa San Michele, a historic villa with beautiful gardens and a small museum.

For families interested in marine life, a visit to the Marine Protected Area of Punta Campanella is a must. Located near the town of Massa Lubrense, this protected area offers snorkeling and diving opportunities that allow visitors to explore the underwater world of the Amalfi Coast. Families can see a variety of marine species, including colorful fish, sea urchins, and octopuses. The area is also home to several ancient shipwrecks, adding an element of adventure and discovery to the experience. Guided snorkeling and diving tours are available, providing equipment and instruction for families with children.

Cooking classes are another excellent activity for families on the Amalfi Coast. Many cooking schools and local chefs offer classes that teach participants how to prepare traditional dishes using fresh, local ingredients. These classes often include a visit to a local market to select ingredients, followed by a hands-on cooking session and a shared meal. Children will enjoy the opportunity to learn new skills and participate in the cooking process. One notable option is Mamma Agata's Cooking School in Ravello, which offers a warm and welcoming environment and teaches participants to prepare a variety of traditional dishes.

Boat rentals and sailing excursions are also popular family activities on the Amalfi Coast. Families can rent a small boat or join a guided sailing tour to explore the coastline, visit hidden beaches, and swim in the clear blue waters of the

Mediterranean Sea. These excursions provide a unique perspective on the region's natural beauty and offer plenty of opportunities for family fun and adventure.

The Amalfi Coast is also home to several festivals and events that are enjoyable for families. The Ravello Festival, held each summer, features classical music concerts and cultural events in the town's beautiful gardens and historic sites. The Festival of San Gennaro in Praiano is another family-friendly event, with processions, fireworks, and traditional music and dance. These festivals provide a lively and festive atmosphere, allowing families to experience the local culture and traditions.

In addition to these specific attractions, the Amalfi Coast offers a variety of family-friendly activities and experiences. Many towns along the coast have local markets where families can shop for fresh produce, handmade crafts, and local specialties. These markets provide a fun and interactive way for children to experience the local culture and cuisine. The vibrant atmosphere and the variety of goods on offer make these markets a delightful experience for families.

For a more hands-on experience, families can visit one of the many artisan workshops in the region. In Vietri sul Mare, known for its ceramics, families can visit workshops where artisans create beautiful hand-painted pottery. Children can watch the artists at work and even participate in a pottery-making class, creating their own unique souvenirs. In

Amalfi, the Paper Museum offers classes in traditional paper-making, allowing families to create beautiful handmade paper using centuries-old methods. These workshops provide a unique and engaging way to connect with the region's artistic heritage.

Outdoor activities are plentiful on the Amalfi Coast, and families can enjoy a variety of adventures together. Hiking is a popular activity, and the Path of the Gods (Sentiero degli Dei) is one of the most famous trails. This hike offers spectacular views of the coastline, the sea, and the surrounding mountains. While the hike can be challenging, it is suitable for older children and teenagers who enjoy outdoor activities. The Path of the Gods is well-marked and provides a sense of adventure and accomplishment for young hikers. Along the way, hikers pass through terraced vineyards, ancient ruins, and charming villages, providing a diverse and enriching experience.

Another excellent outdoor activity is visiting the Valle delle Ferriere, a nature reserve located near Amalfi. The reserve offers several hiking trails that take visitors through lush forests, past waterfalls, and along ancient aqueducts. The trails are well-marked and suitable for families with children of all ages. The Valle delle Ferriere is home to a variety of plant and animal species, and families can learn about the local flora and fauna while enjoying the natural beauty of the area. The reserve also includes the remains of ancient ironworks, adding a historical dimension to the hike.

For families seeking adventure on the water, kayaking and paddleboarding are great options. Several rental shops along the coast offer kayaks and paddleboards, and guided tours are also available. These activities provide a fun and exciting way to explore the coastline and enjoy the crystal-clear waters of the Mediterranean Sea. Children will love the thrill of paddling through the waves and discovering hidden coves and beaches.

Each activity provides a unique and enriching experience, allowing families to immerse themselves in the beauty, culture, and traditions of the Amalfi Coast. Whether you are seeking adventure, relaxation, or educational enrichment, the Amalfi Coast provides the perfect backdrop for a family-friendly and memorable getaway.

Best Family Accommodations

Finding the perfect family accommodation on the Amalfi Coast is key to ensuring a comfortable and enjoyable trip. The region offers a variety of options that cater to families, from luxurious hotels and resorts to charming villas and apartments. Each type of accommodation has its own unique features and benefits, providing something to suit every family's needs and preferences.

One of the top choices for family accommodations on the Amalfi Coast is the Hotel Santa Caterina in Amalfi. This luxurious hotel offers a perfect blend of elegance and comfort, making it an ideal choice for families. The hotel features spacious family rooms and suites that provide plenty of space for everyone to relax and unwind. Many of the rooms offer stunning views of the sea, and some even come with private terraces. The hotel's amenities include a heated outdoor pool, a private beach, and beautiful gardens, providing plenty of opportunities for family fun and relaxation. The Hotel Santa Caterina also offers a variety of dining options, including a restaurant that serves delicious Mediterranean cuisine made with fresh, local ingredients.

Another excellent option in Amalfi is the NH Collection Grand Hotel Convento di Amalfi. This historic hotel, housed in a former monastery, offers a unique and enchanting setting for a family stay. The hotel features family rooms and suites that are both spacious and comfortable, ensuring that everyone has plenty of room to relax. The NH Collection Grand Hotel Convento di Amalfi also offers a range of amenities, including an infinity pool, a fitness center, and a spa. The hotel's restaurant serves a variety of Italian and international dishes, making it easy to find something to suit everyone's tastes. The central location of the hotel provides easy access to the town's many attractions, shops, and restaurants.

In Positano, the Le Sirenuse Hotel is a top choice for families seeking luxury and comfort. This iconic hotel offers a range of family-friendly accommodations, including spacious suites and connecting rooms. The hotel's amenities include a beautiful outdoor pool, a spa, and a fitness center. The Le Sirenuse Hotel also offers a variety of dining options, including a Michelin-starred restaurant that serves exquisite Mediterranean cuisine. The hotel's central location in Positano provides easy access to the town's main beach, shops, and restaurants, making it a convenient and enjoyable choice for families.

For families looking for a more intimate and charming experience, the Hotel Villa Franca in Positano is an excellent option. This boutique hotel offers a range of family-friendly accommodations, including suites and connecting rooms. The hotel's amenities include a rooftop pool, a spa, and a fitness center. The Hotel Villa Franca also offers a variety of dining options, including a restaurant that serves delicious Italian cuisine made with fresh, local ingredients. The hotel's central location provides easy access to Positano's many attractions, shops, and restaurants, making it a convenient and enjoyable choice for families.

Another top choice for family accommodations in Positano is the Hotel Poseidon. This charming hotel offers a range of family-friendly accommodations, including spacious rooms and suites with stunning views of the sea. The hotel's amenities include an outdoor pool, a fitness center, and a spa. The Hotel Poseidon also offers a variety of dining options, including a restaurant that serves delicious Mediterranean cuisine made with fresh, local ingredients. The hotel's central location provides easy access to Positano's main beach, shops, and restaurants, making it a convenient and enjoyable choice for families.

In Ravello, the Belmond Hotel Caruso is a top choice for families seeking luxury and elegance. This historic hotel, set in a beautifully restored 11th-century building, offers a range of family-friendly accommodations, including spacious rooms and suites with stunning views of the sea and the surrounding gardens. The hotel's amenities include an infinity pool, a fitness center, and a spa. The Belmond Hotel Caruso also offers a variety of dining options, including a restaurant that serves exquisite Italian cuisine made with fresh, local ingredients. The hotel's central location provides easy access to Ravello's many attractions, shops, and restaurants, making it a convenient and enjoyable choice for families.

Another excellent option in Ravello is the Palazzo Avino. This luxurious hotel offers a range of family-friendly accommodations, including spacious rooms and suites with stunning views of the sea and the surrounding gardens. The hotel's amenities include an outdoor pool, a fitness center, and a spa. The Palazzo Avino also offers a variety of dining options, including a Michelin-starred restaurant that serves exquisite Italian cuisine made with fresh, local ingredients. The hotel's central location provides easy access to Ravello's many attractions, shops, and restaurants, making it a convenient and enjoyable choice for families.

In Maiori, the Hotel Club Due Torri is a top choice for families seeking a comfortable and relaxed stay. This family-friendly hotel offers a range of accommodations, including spacious rooms and suites with stunning views of the sea. The hotel's amenities include an outdoor pool, a private beach, and a fitness center. The Hotel Club Due Torri also offers a variety of dining options, including a restaurant that serves delicious Italian cuisine made with fresh, local ingredients. The hotel's central location provides easy access to Maiori's many attractions, shops, and restaurants, making it a convenient and enjoyable choice for families.

For families looking for a more intimate and charming experience in Maiori, the Hotel Pietra di Luna is an excellent option. This boutique hotel offers a range of family-friendly accommodations, including spacious rooms and suites with stunning views of the sea. The hotel's amenities include an outdoor pool, a private beach, and a fitness center. The Hotel Pietra di Luna also offers a variety of dining options, including a restaurant that serves delicious Italian cuisine made with fresh, local ingredients. The hotel's central location provides easy access to Maiori's many attractions, shops, and restaurants, making it a convenient and enjoyable choice for families.

In Minori, the Hotel Santa Lucia is a top choice for families seeking a comfortable and relaxed stay. This family-friendly hotel offers a range of accommodations, including spacious rooms and suites with stunning views of the sea. The hotel's amenities include an outdoor pool, a private beach, and a fitness center. The Hotel Santa Lucia also offers a variety of dining options, including a restaurant that serves delicious Italian cuisine made with fresh, local ingredients. The hotel's central location provides easy access to Minori's many attractions, shops, and restaurants, making it a convenient and enjoyable choice for families.

Another excellent option in Minori is the Villa Romana Hotel & Spa. This charming hotel offers a range of family-friendly accommodations, including spacious rooms and suites with stunning views of the sea and the surrounding gardens. The hotel's amenities include an outdoor pool, a fitness center, and a spa. The Villa Romana Hotel & Spa also offers a variety of dining options, including a restaurant that serves delicious Italian cuisine made with fresh, local ingredients. The hotel's central location provides easy access to Minori's many attractions, shops, and restaurants, making it a convenient and enjoyable choice for families.

The Amalfi Coast offers a wide range of family accommodations that cater to all tastes and preferences. From luxurious hotels and resorts to charming boutique hotels and apartments, there is something to suit every family's needs. Each accommodation provides a unique and enjoyable experience, allowing families to relax and unwind while exploring the beauty, culture, and traditions of the Amalfi Coast. Whether you are seeking a luxurious stay with stunning views or a more intimate and charming experience, the Amalfi Coast provides the perfect backdrop for a family-friendly and memorable getaway.

CHAPTER 13

DAY TRIPS AND NEARBY EXCURSIONS

Day Trips to Nearby Islands

Day trips to nearby islands offer a wonderful opportunity to explore more of the stunning beauty and rich culture that the Amalfi Coast region has to offer. The islands of Capri, Ischia, and Procida each provide unique experiences, making them perfect destinations for a memorable day trip.

Starting with Capri, this island is perhaps the most famous and frequently visited of the three. Known for its rugged landscape, upscale shopping, and stunning views, Capri is a must-visit for anyone traveling to the Amalfi Coast. The journey to Capri is itself a delightful experience, with ferry and boat services regularly departing from various towns along the coast, including Positano, Amalfi, and Sorrento. The boat ride to Capri offers breathtaking views of the coastline and the open sea, setting the stage for a wonderful day.

Upon arrival in Capri, one of the first places to visit is the town of Capri itself. The town is filled with charming streets, high-end boutiques, and quaint cafes. A visit to the Piazzetta, the main square, is a must. This lively area is often referred to as the "living room" of Capri, where locals and tourists gather to enjoy a coffee or an aperitif while taking in the vibrant atmosphere. The narrow streets around the Piazzetta are lined with luxury shops and designer boutiques, perfect for those looking to indulge in some shopping.

For those interested in natural beauty, a visit to the Blue Grotto (Grotta Azzurra) is essential. This sea cave is famous for its stunning blue light, which is created by sunlight passing through an underwater cavity and shining through the seawater. Visitors can take small rowboats into the grotto, where they can marvel at the magical blue glow. It is worth noting that the Blue Grotto can be very popular, so it is advisable to visit early in the day to avoid the crowds.

Another highlight of Capri is the chairlift to Monte Solaro, the highest point on the island. The chairlift departs from Anacapri, a quieter and more laid-back town compared to Capri. The ride to the top offers spectacular views of the island and the sea, and the summit provides panoramic vistas that are truly breathtaking. Monte Solaro is an excellent spot for taking photos and enjoying the natural beauty of Capri.

Anacapri itself is worth exploring. This charming town is home to the Villa San Michele, a historic villa built by the Swedish physician and author Axel Munthe. The villa features beautiful gardens, ancient artifacts, and stunning views of the sea and the surrounding landscape. The peaceful and serene atmosphere of Villa San Michele makes it a perfect place to relax and unwind.

For a more adventurous experience, families can hike along the Pizzolungo trail, which offers stunning views of the coastline and the famous Faraglioni rock formations. This trail takes visitors through scenic landscapes and offers numerous photo opportunities. The trail is relatively easy and suitable for families with older children who enjoy hiking.

Next, we have the island of Ischia, known for its thermal springs, lush gardens, and beautiful beaches. Like Capri, Ischia is easily accessible by ferry from various towns along the Amalfi Coast. The island is larger than Capri and offers a more diverse range of activities and attractions.

One of the main draws of Ischia is its thermal baths. The island is home to numerous thermal parks and spas, where visitors can relax and rejuvenate in the healing waters. One of the most popular thermal parks is the Poseidon Gardens, located in Forio. This extensive park features a variety of thermal pools, saunas, and relaxation areas, all set within beautifully landscaped gardens. The thermal waters are believed to have therapeutic properties, making this a perfect place to unwind and recharge.

For families, a visit to the Negombo Thermal Park in Lacco Ameno is highly recommended. This park offers a range of thermal pools, water slides, and play areas that are perfect for children. The park also has a private beach where families can relax and enjoy the sun and sea.

Ischia is also known for its stunning gardens. The La Mortella Gardens, created by the English composer Sir William Walton and his wife Susana, are a must-see. These gardens feature a wide variety of exotic plants, water features, and sculptures, all set within a lush and tranquil environment. The gardens also host classical music concerts, providing a unique cultural experience.

For history enthusiasts, a visit to the Aragonese Castle is essential. This medieval castle is located on a small islet connected to Ischia by a causeway. The castle offers stunning views of the island and the sea and is home to several museums and exhibitions. Visitors can explore the castle's ancient walls, towers, and chapels, learning about the island's rich history.

Lastly, the island of Procida, the smallest of the three islands, offers a more authentic and tranquil experience. Procida is less touristy than Capri and Ischia, making it a perfect destination for those looking to escape the crowds and enjoy a more relaxed atmosphere.

The main town of Procida, with its colorful buildings and narrow streets, is a delight to explore. The Marina Corricella, the island's main harbor, is particularly picturesque, with its pastel-colored houses and fishing boats. This area is perfect for a leisurely stroll, and there are several cafes and restaurants where visitors can enjoy fresh seafood and local specialties.

For a unique and educational experience, families can visit the Terra Murata, a historic fortified village located on the highest point of the island. The village offers stunning views of the sea and the surrounding islands and is home to several historical buildings, including the Abbey of San Michele Arcangelo. Visitors can explore the narrow streets and ancient walls, learning about the island's history and culture.

Procida is also home to several beautiful beaches, such as the Chiaiolella Beach and the Pozzo Vecchio Beach. These beaches offer crystal-clear waters and soft sand, perfect for swimming and sunbathing. The relaxed and unspoiled atmosphere of Procida's beaches makes them ideal for families looking to enjoy a peaceful day by the sea.

Day trips to the nearby islands of Capri, Ischia, and Procida offer a wealth of experiences for visitors to the Amalfi Coast. Each island has its own unique charm and attractions, providing something for everyone. From the upscale shopping and stunning natural beauty of Capri to the thermal baths and lush gardens of Ischia, and the authentic and tranquil atmosphere of Procida, there is no shortage of activities and sights to enjoy. These day trips provide an excellent opportunity to explore more of the region's beauty, culture, and history, creating unforgettable memories for families and travelers alike.

CHAPTER 14

PRACTICAL INFORMATION

Emergency Contacts and Numbers

When traveling to a new place, it's essential to be prepared for any unexpected situations that may arise. Knowing the emergency contacts and numbers for the Amalfi Coast can be a lifesaver in case of emergencies.

First and foremost, the general emergency number in Italy is 112. This is the equivalent of 911 in the United States and can be used for any type of emergency, including medical, fire, and police. When you call 112, you will be connected to an operator who can direct your call to the appropriate emergency service. It's important to know that operators can assist you in multiple languages, including English, which is helpful for international travelers.

For medical emergencies, the number to call is 118. This number connects you to the medical emergency services, where you can request an ambulance or get assistance for any urgent health issues. The operators are trained to handle a wide range of medical situations and can provide instructions on what to do until help arrives. It's crucial to provide clear and concise information about your location and the nature of the emergency to ensure a swift response.

In case of a fire, the number to call is 115. This will connect you to the fire department, which can respond to any fire-related emergencies, including fires in buildings, forest fires, and other hazardous situations. The fire department is equipped to handle a variety of emergencies and can also assist with rescue operations if needed.

If you need to contact the police for any reason, including reporting a crime or seeking assistance, the number to call is 113. The police can help with a wide range of issues, from theft and assault to lost property and general safety concerns. It's important to provide detailed information about the situation and your location when calling the police to ensure they can respond effectively.

For issues related to maritime emergencies, such as problems on a boat or incidents at sea, the number to call is 1530. This connects you to the Italian Coast Guard, which can assist with search and rescue operations, maritime safety, and other emergencies on the water. The Coast Guard is equipped to handle a variety of maritime situations and can provide assistance quickly.

In addition to these primary emergency numbers, there are several other important contacts to be aware of when visiting the Amalfi Coast. One of these is the local health service, known as Guardia Medica. The Guardia Medica provides non-emergency medical assistance and can be reached at various numbers depending on your location. They can assist with minor medical issues, provide prescriptions, and offer general health advice.

For travelers with specific health needs, it's also important to know the location of the nearest hospitals and clinics. The Amalfi Coast is served by several hospitals, including the Ospedale di Salerno, which is the main hospital in the region. This hospital is equipped to handle a wide range of medical emergencies and has an emergency room that operates 24/7. Other hospitals in the area include the Ospedale di Nocera Inferiore and the Ospedale di Cava de' Tirreni. Knowing the locations of these hospitals and how to get there can be very helpful in case of a medical emergency.

Pharmacies are another important resource for travelers. In Italy, pharmacies can provide over-the-counter medications, medical supplies, and advice for minor health issues. Many pharmacies also have a green cross sign that lights up to indicate they are open. It's useful to know the location of the nearest pharmacy to your accommodation and their opening hours. Some pharmacies also offer a night service (farmacia di turno), where you can obtain medications outside of regular hours.

For travelers with young children, it's important to have contact information for pediatricians and child health services. Many towns along the Amalfi Coast have pediatricians who can provide medical care for children. Additionally, the Ospedale Pediatrico Santobono in Naples is a specialized children's hospital that can handle more serious pediatric cases.

In case of a car accident or other roadside emergencies, the number to call is 803116, which connects you to the Automobile Club d'Italia (ACI). The ACI provides roadside assistance and can help with issues such as breakdowns, flat tires, and other vehicle-related problems. They can also arrange for towing services if needed.

For travelers who may need assistance with legal issues, it's important to have contact information for local consulates and embassies. The consulates can provide assistance with issues such as lost passports, legal problems, and other emergencies that may arise while traveling. The contact information for your country's consulate or embassy can usually be found online, and it's a good idea to have this information readily available.

For those who may need assistance with language barriers or other travel-related issues, the Italian Tourist Assistance Service (ENIT) can be a valuable resource. They can provide information and assistance in multiple languages and help with a wide range of travel-related issues.

It's also a good idea to have contact information for your accommodation and any local contacts you may have. This can be helpful in case you need assistance or have an emergency situation. Many hotels and rental properties provide emergency contact numbers for their guests, including local doctors, emergency services, and staff who can assist with various issues.

Being prepared with the right emergency contacts and numbers is crucial when traveling to the Amalfi Coast. Knowing who to call and having the necessary information can make a significant difference in how quickly and effectively you can respond to an emergency situation. By familiarizing yourself with these contacts and keeping the information readily available, you can ensure a safer and more enjoyable trip to this beautiful region. Whether you are dealing with a medical emergency, a fire, a crime, or any other situation, knowing the right numbers to call and the services available can provide peace of mind and help you navigate any challenges that may arise during your travels.

Health Care and Medical Services

Healthcare and medical services on the Amalfi Coast are well-established and provide comprehensive care to both residents and visitors. Understanding the available services and how to access them is essential for anyone planning to spend time in this beautiful region.

Italy has a highly regarded healthcare system, known for its high-quality medical care and accessibility. The Amalfi Coast, though relatively remote, benefits from this national healthcare framework. The region is equipped with a variety of medical facilities, including hospitals, clinics, pharmacies, and specialized care centers, all designed to meet the needs of the local population and the many tourists who visit each year.

Hospitals are a crucial part of the healthcare infrastructure on the Amalfi Coast. The main hospital serving the region is the Ospedale di Salerno, located in the city of Salerno. This hospital is a large, full-service facility equipped with an emergency department that operates 24/7, intensive care units, surgical departments, and various medical specialties. The hospital's emergency department is staffed with trained professionals who can handle a wide range of medical emergencies, from trauma and cardiac events to minor injuries and illnesses.

In addition to the Ospedale di Salerno, there are other hospitals in the region, such as the Ospedale di Nocera Inferiore and the Ospedale di Cava de' Tirreni. These hospitals also provide comprehensive medical services and have emergency departments that can treat urgent medical conditions. Knowing the locations of these hospitals and how to get there is crucial for anyone staying on the Amalfi Coast, as it ensures that help is readily available in case of an emergency.

For less urgent medical needs, the Guardia Medica, or local health service, is available. The Guardia Medica provides non-emergency medical assistance, such as treating minor illnesses and injuries, providing prescriptions, and offering general health advice. Each town along the Amalfi Coast has access to these services, and they can be reached through various contact numbers depending on your specific location. The Guardia Medica is especially useful for travelers who may need medical attention outside of regular hospital hours or for conditions that do not require a visit to the emergency room.

Pharmacies are another critical component of the healthcare system on the Amalfi Coast. Italian pharmacies, identifiable by a green cross sign, are well-stocked with over-the-counter medications, medical supplies, and prescription drugs. Pharmacists in Italy are highly trained and can provide advice on minor health issues, recommend treatments, and dispense medications. Most towns along the Amalfi Coast have at least one pharmacy, and it is beneficial to know their locations and opening hours. Some pharmacies also offer a night service (farmacia di turno), ensuring that you can obtain necessary medications outside of regular business hours.

In addition to pharmacies, there are numerous private clinics and medical practices along the Amalfi Coast. These clinics offer a range of medical services, including general practice, pediatrics, dermatology, and other specialties. Many of these clinics cater specifically to tourists and offer services in multiple languages, including English. Visiting a private clinic can be a convenient option for non-emergency medical care, and appointments can often be scheduled on short notice.

For those traveling with children, access to pediatric care is an important consideration. Pediatricians are available in various towns along the Amalfi Coast and can provide medical care for infants, children, and adolescents. The Ospedale Pediatrico Santobono in Naples is a specialized children's hospital that can handle more serious pediatric cases and provides comprehensive medical services for young patients.

Dental care is also readily available on the Amalfi Coast. There are numerous dental clinics and practices that offer a range of services, from routine check-ups and cleanings to emergency dental care and more complex procedures. As with other medical services, many dental clinics cater to tourists and offer services in multiple languages.

In case of emergencies, it is essential to know the appropriate contact numbers. The general emergency number in Italy is 112, which can be used for any type of emergency, including medical, fire, and police. For medical emergencies specifically, the number to call is 118. This connects you to the medical emergency services, where you can request an ambulance or get assistance for urgent health issues. Providing clear information about your location and the nature of the emergency is crucial to ensure a swift response.

For maritime emergencies, which can be relevant given the coastal nature of the region, the number to call is 1530. This connects you to the Italian Coast Guard, which can assist with incidents at sea, search and rescue operations, and other maritime emergencies.

Travel insurance is another important aspect to consider when traveling to the Amalfi Coast. While the healthcare system in Italy is excellent, having travel insurance can provide additional peace of mind and cover expenses for medical treatment, emergency evacuation, and other unforeseen events. It is advisable to choose a travel insurance plan that includes comprehensive medical coverage and to carry a copy of your insurance policy and contact information with you at all times.

In addition to traditional medical services, the Amalfi Coast also offers various wellness and spa facilities. These establishments provide services such as massages, facials, and other treatments designed to promote relaxation and well-being. Many hotels and resorts along the coast have their own wellness centers, offering a convenient way to unwind and take care of your health while enjoying your stay.

For travelers with specific medical needs, such as those requiring regular medication or treatment, it is important to plan ahead. Ensure that you bring an adequate supply of any necessary medications, along with copies of your prescriptions. It can also be helpful to have a letter from your doctor outlining your medical condition and the treatments you require. This information can be invaluable if you need to seek medical care while abroad.

Healthcare and medical services on the Amalfi Coast are well-equipped to handle the needs of both residents and visitors. By familiarizing yourself with the available services and knowing how to access them, you can ensure that you are prepared for any medical situation that may arise during your stay. Whether you need emergency care, routine medical treatment, or advice for minor health issues, the healthcare system on the Amalfi Coast is designed to provide comprehensive and accessible care, ensuring that your trip is as safe and enjoyable as possible.

Accessibility Information

The Amalfi Coast, with its stunning landscapes, historic towns, and vibrant culture, is a dream destination for many travelers. However, the region's rugged terrain, steep cliffs, and narrow, winding streets can pose significant challenges for those with mobility issues or other disabilities.

Traveling to the Amalfi Coast requires careful planning, especially for those with accessibility needs. The first step in ensuring a smooth and enjoyable trip is to choose the right transportation. The region is accessible by car, bus, ferry, and train, each with its own set of considerations for accessibility.

Arriving by car is one of the most flexible options for those with mobility issues. Renting a car allows travelers to move at their own pace and provides easier access to remote areas that may be difficult to reach by public transportation. However, it's important to note that the roads along the Amalfi Coast are narrow and winding, with limited parking in many towns. For those who require accessible vehicles, several car rental companies offer cars with features such as hand controls, wheelchair lifts, and extra space for mobility devices. Booking these vehicles in advance is highly recommended to ensure availability.

Public buses operated by the SITA bus company are another option for getting around the Amalfi Coast. While buses are a cost-effective way to travel, they can be crowded, especially during peak tourist season. Not all buses are fully accessible, but some are equipped with low floors and ramps to accommodate wheelchairs. It's advisable to check the specific accessibility features of the buses in advance and plan your trips during off-peak times to avoid crowds.

Ferries provide a scenic and enjoyable way to travel between coastal towns. The main ferry operators, including Travelmar and Alilauro, offer services that connect towns like Amalfi, Positano, and Salerno. While ferries can be more accessible than buses due to their spacious decks, it's important to check with the ferry operators about the accessibility features of each vessel. Some ferries have ramps and designated spaces for wheelchairs, while others may have steps that can be difficult to navigate.

For those arriving by train, the nearest major station is in Salerno, which is connected to the Amalfi Coast by bus or ferry. Salerno's train station is relatively accessible, with elevators and ramps available for passengers with mobility issues. From Salerno, travelers can take accessible buses or ferries to their final destination along the coast.

Once on the Amalfi Coast, navigating the towns can be challenging due to the steep terrain and narrow streets. However, some towns are more accessible than others. Amalfi, for example, has a relatively flat town center with several accessible attractions, shops, and restaurants. The Cathedral of Amalfi, while situated on a hill, has a stair lift available to assist visitors with mobility issues. The main piazza and surrounding streets are mostly level and can be navigated with a wheelchair or mobility scooter.

Positano, known for its steep streets and numerous steps, can be more challenging for those with mobility issues. However, the town's main beach, Spiaggia Grande, is accessible via a level pathway from the main road. Additionally, some hotels and restaurants in Positano have made efforts to improve accessibility by installing ramps and providing accessible facilities. It's important to communicate with accommodation providers in advance to ensure that they can meet your specific needs.

Ravello, perched high above the coast, offers stunning views and beautiful gardens. While the town itself is less accessible due to its hilly terrain and many steps, some attractions, such as Villa Rufolo, have made efforts to accommodate visitors with disabilities. Villa Rufolo has ramps and accessible pathways that allow visitors to explore its gardens and enjoy the panoramic views.

Maiori and Minori are two towns that are relatively flat and more accessible than other areas along the coast. Maiori's long promenade and sandy beach are easily navigable, and the town has several accessible restaurants and shops. Minori also offers a flat town center with accessible pathways, making it a good option for travelers with mobility issues.

Accommodations on the Amalfi Coast vary widely in terms of accessibility. Many hotels and vacation rentals are located in historic buildings that may have steps and narrow doorways, but there are also properties that have been adapted to be more accessible. When booking accommodation, it's essential to communicate your specific needs to the property owners or managers. Look for hotels that offer features such as ground-floor rooms, elevators, roll-in showers, and grab bars in bathrooms. Some hotels also provide accessible transportation services to help guests get around the area.

In addition to accommodations, dining options on the Amalfi Coast can vary in terms of accessibility. Many restaurants are located on steep streets or have steps leading to their entrances. However, there are also many accessible dining options available. Restaurants with outdoor seating often provide more accessible entrances and spaces for wheelchairs. When making reservations, it's a good idea to inquire about accessibility features and request seating that meets your needs.

For travelers with visual or hearing impairments, accessibility features such as Braille menus, audio guides, and sign language interpreters may not be widely available. However, some museums and cultural sites offer accessible resources, and it's worth inquiring in advance. Bringing assistive devices, such as portable ramps, magnifiers, or hearing aids, can also help enhance accessibility during your trip.

Medical facilities on the Amalfi Coast are equipped to handle a variety of health needs, including emergencies. The main hospital in the region, Ospedale di Salerno, has facilities and services to accommodate patients with disabilities. Pharmacies are also widely available and can provide over-the-counter medications, medical supplies, and advice. Knowing the location of the nearest hospital and pharmacy to your accommodation can provide peace of mind in case of any health issues.

Traveling with a companion or caregiver can significantly enhance the accessibility and enjoyment of your trip. Having someone to assist with navigating the terrain, carrying luggage, and providing support can make a big difference. Many travel companies offer guided tours that cater to travelers with disabilities, providing accessible transportation, accommodations, and activities. These tours can be an excellent way to explore the Amalfi Coast without worrying about the logistical challenges.

While the Amalfi Coast presents some accessibility challenges due to its steep terrain and historic infrastructure, careful planning and preparation can help ensure a smooth and enjoyable trip. By understanding the available transportation options, choosing accessible accommodations, and communicating your needs with service providers, you can experience the beauty and culture of the Amalfi Coast with confidence. Whether you're exploring the charming streets of Amalfi, relaxing on the beaches of Maiori, or enjoying the views from Ravello, the Amalfi Coast offers a wealth of experiences that can be enjoyed by all travelers, including those with disabilities.

Local Customs and Laws

Understanding the local customs and laws of the Amalfi Coast is essential for anyone planning to visit this beautiful region. This knowledge not only helps ensure a respectful and enjoyable trip but also aids in navigating the social and legal landscape effectively.

The Amalfi Coast, located in southern Italy, is renowned for its stunning coastal scenery, historic towns, and rich cultural heritage. The region's customs and traditions are deeply rooted in its history and way of life. Respecting these customs is important for visitors to fully appreciate the local culture and interact harmoniously with the residents.

One of the most important aspects of Italian culture is the emphasis on family and social relationships. Family gatherings and meals are central to daily life, and showing respect for these traditions is appreciated. When visiting local restaurants or staying with host families, it is customary to engage in conversations and show interest in the lives and experiences of the people you meet. Italians often greet each other with a kiss on both cheeks, even when meeting for the first time. This gesture is a sign of friendliness and warmth, and it is polite to reciprocate.

Dining customs on the Amalfi Coast are an integral part of the local culture. Meals are often leisurely and social events, with multiple courses and plenty of time for conversation. It is common to start with antipasti (appetizers), followed by primi (first courses such as pasta or risotto), secondi (main courses, typically meat or fish), contorni (side dishes), and dolci (desserts). Wine is frequently enjoyed with meals, and it is polite to wait for the host to make the first toast before drinking. Tipping in restaurants is not obligatory but is appreciated; leaving a small amount of change or rounding up the bill is customary.

Dress code is another important consideration when visiting the Amalfi Coast. While casual attire is acceptable for most daytime activities, Italians tend to dress more formally in the evenings and for dining out. Wearing appropriate clothing when visiting churches and religious sites is also important. Shoulders and knees should be covered, and hats should be removed upon entering. This shows respect for the sacredness of these places and aligns with local expectations.

Shopping and market visits are popular activities on the Amalfi Coast. When purchasing items from local markets or shops, it is customary to greet the shopkeeper with a friendly "buongiorno" (good morning) or "buonasera" (good evening). Bargaining is not common in Italy, and prices are usually fixed. However, it is acceptable to ask for a small discount, especially if you are buying multiple items. Paying with cash is preferred in smaller shops and markets, although credit cards are widely accepted in larger establishments.

Public behavior and social etiquette are also important to consider. Italians value politeness and courteous behavior in public settings. Speaking in a moderate tone and avoiding loud or disruptive behavior is appreciated. When using public transportation, it is customary to offer your seat to elderly passengers, pregnant women, and people with disabilities. Smoking is prohibited in public places such as restaurants, bars, and public transport, and designated smoking areas should be used.

Respect for the environment is a significant aspect of life on the Amalfi Coast. The region's natural beauty is one of its greatest assets, and locals take great pride in preserving it. Visitors are expected to follow environmental regulations, such as disposing of trash properly, recycling when possible, and not disturbing wildlife. It is also important to respect designated protected areas and follow guidelines for activities such as hiking and swimming to minimize impact on the environment.

When it comes to local laws, Italy has specific regulations that visitors should be aware of. One key area is driving laws. The roads along the Amalfi Coast can be narrow and winding, with limited visibility in some areas. Speed limits and road signs should be strictly adhered to, and driving under the influence of alcohol is illegal. The legal blood alcohol limit in Italy is 0.05%, which is lower than in many other countries. It is advisable to avoid drinking if you plan to drive. Seat belts are mandatory for all passengers, and children under 12 years old must use appropriate child safety seats.

Another important legal consideration is the requirement to carry identification at all times. Visitors are required to carry their passport or a copy of it, along with any relevant travel documents. This is especially important when checking into hotels, where identification is needed for registration. It is also advisable to carry a photocopy of your passport and leave the original in a secure place, such as a hotel safe, to avoid the risk of loss or theft.

Visitors should also be aware of the laws regarding alcohol consumption in public places. While it is common to enjoy a glass of wine or beer with a meal, consuming alcohol in public spaces such as parks, streets, and beaches is generally prohibited. This regulation is enforced to maintain public order and ensure the safety of residents and visitors.

Beach etiquette is another important aspect of local customs on the Amalfi Coast. Many of the beaches are privately owned and require a fee for access. These private beaches offer amenities such as sun loungers, umbrellas, and changing facilities. Public beaches are also available and are typically free to access, but they may have fewer facilities. It is important to respect the rules of both private and public beaches, such as not leaving trash behind, not playing loud music, and respecting the personal space of other beachgoers.

Cultural events and festivals are an integral part of life on the Amalfi Coast, and participating in these events can provide a deeper understanding of local customs and traditions. Festivals often include religious processions, music, dancing, and traditional foods. Showing respect for these cultural celebrations, whether as a participant or an observer, is important. It is advisable to follow the lead of local residents, dress appropriately for the occasion, and participate with an open and respectful attitude.

In addition to cultural customs, understanding basic Italian phrases and expressions can greatly enhance your experience on the Amalfi Coast. While many locals speak English, especially in tourist areas, making an effort to speak Italian is appreciated. Simple greetings such as "ciao" (hello), "grazie" (thank you), and "per favore" (please) can go a long way in showing respect and building rapport with locals. Learning a few key phrases can also help in practical situations, such as ordering food, asking for directions, or making purchases.

Respecting privacy and personal space is another important aspect of local customs. Italians value their personal space and privacy, and it is important to be mindful of this in social interactions. Avoiding intrusive questions, giving people space, and being polite in conversations are all ways to show respect for local customs.

Understanding and respecting the local customs and laws of the Amalfi Coast is essential for a successful and enjoyable trip. By familiarizing yourself with these customs, you can navigate the social and legal landscape effectively, build positive relationships with locals, and fully appreciate the rich culture and traditions of the region. Whether you are dining at a local restaurant, exploring historic sites, or participating in a cultural festival, showing respect for local customs and laws will enhance your experience and ensure a memorable visit to this beautiful part of Italy.

Internet and Communication

The Amalfi Coast, renowned for its picturesque scenery, rich history, and vibrant culture, also offers a range of modern conveniences, including internet and communication services.

Staying connected while traveling is essential for various reasons, including keeping in touch with family and friends, accessing important information, navigating, and sharing travel experiences. The Amalfi Coast, despite its rugged terrain and historic towns, has made significant strides in providing reliable internet and communication services to residents and tourists alike.

The primary means of accessing the internet on the Amalfi Coast is through Wi-Fi. Most hotels, resorts, and vacation rentals offer free Wi-Fi to their guests. The quality and speed of the Wi-Fi connection can vary depending on the location and the specific accommodation. In larger towns such as Amalfi, Positano, and Ravello, you can generally expect a stable and reasonably fast connection. However, in more remote areas, the connection may be slower and less reliable. It is always a good idea to check with your accommodation provider about the availability and quality of Wi-Fi before booking.

In addition to accommodations, many cafes, restaurants, and public spaces offer free Wi-Fi. These establishments often display signs indicating the availability of Wi-Fi, and the staff can provide you with the password upon request. Using Wi-Fi at these locations can be a convenient way to stay connected while enjoying a meal or a coffee. It's important to note that while public Wi-Fi is widely available, it may not always be secure. Avoid accessing sensitive information, such as banking details, over public networks to ensure your privacy and security.

For those who require a more reliable and secure internet connection, mobile data is an excellent option. Italy has several major mobile network providers, including TIM, Vodafone, Wind Tre, and Iliad, which offer extensive coverage across the country, including the Amalfi Coast. Visitors can purchase a local SIM card upon arrival in Italy. These SIM cards are available at airports, mobile phone shops, and convenience stores. Using a local SIM card can be a cost-effective way to access the internet, make phone calls, and send text messages without incurring high roaming charges from your home country's provider.

When purchasing a SIM card, you will need to provide identification, such as a passport. SIM cards can be purchased with a variety of plans, including pay-as-you-go options and pre-paid bundles that include a set amount of data, call minutes, and text messages. It's advisable to compare the different plans available and choose one that best suits your needs. Some providers also offer tourist-specific plans that are tailored to short-term visitors and include generous data allowances.

For travelers who prefer to use their own devices without changing SIM cards, portable Wi-Fi devices, also known as pocket Wi-Fi or mobile hotspots, are a convenient alternative. These devices provide a secure and reliable internet connection that can be shared among multiple devices, such as smartphones, tablets, and laptops. Portable Wi-Fi devices can be rented from various companies online and delivered to your accommodation or picked up at the airport. This option is particularly useful for families or groups traveling together, as it allows multiple people to stay connected using a single device.

In terms of mobile network coverage, the Amalfi Coast is generally well-served by Italy's major providers. However, the region's mountainous terrain and narrow valleys can sometimes result in spotty coverage, particularly in more remote or less populated areas. In towns and along the main roads, you can expect a good signal and reliable service. It's a good idea to check the coverage maps provided by mobile network operators to ensure that you will have adequate service in the areas you plan to visit.

When it comes to making phone calls, using a local SIM card or a portable Wi-Fi device with a voice-over-internet-protocol (VoIP) app, such as Skype, WhatsApp, or Viber, can be a cost-effective way to stay in touch with friends and family back home. These apps use your internet connection to make calls and send messages, avoiding the high costs associated with international roaming charges. Many of these apps also offer video calling, which can be a great way to share your travel experiences with loved ones.

For those who need to send or receive important documents, fax services are available at some hotels, business centers, and post offices. While faxing is less common in the digital age, it can still be a useful option for certain types of communication. Additionally, many hotels and accommodations offer printing and scanning services, which can be helpful for travelers who need to print tickets, itineraries, or other important documents.

Postal services on the Amalfi Coast are reliable and efficient, allowing you to send postcards, letters, and packages to friends and family. Post offices are located in most towns, and they offer a range of services, including express mail, registered mail, and parcel shipping. Postage stamps can also be purchased at tobacco shops (tabaccherie), which are marked with a blue or white "T" sign.

Language can sometimes be a barrier when accessing communication services, but many locals and service providers on the Amalfi Coast speak English, especially in tourist areas. However, learning a few basic Italian phrases can be helpful and is often appreciated by the locals. Simple phrases such as "Posso avere la password del Wi-Fi?" (Can I have the Wi-Fi password?) or "Dove posso comprare una scheda SIM?" (Where can I buy a SIM card?) can go a long way in making your interactions smoother and more enjoyable.

For those who need to stay connected for work purposes, co-working spaces and business centers are available in some of the larger towns on the Amalfi Coast. These spaces provide a quiet and professional environment with high-speed internet, meeting rooms, and office amenities. Using a co-working space can be an excellent option for digital nomads or business travelers who need a reliable place to work.

The Amalfi Coast offers a variety of internet and communication options to ensure that visitors can stay connected during their trip. From free Wi-Fi in accommodations and public spaces to mobile data plans and portable Wi-Fi devices, there are solutions to meet the needs of every traveler. Understanding the available options and planning ahead can help you make the most of your time on the Amalfi Coast while staying connected with the world. Whether you need to check emails, navigate the area, share your travel experiences, or keep in touch with loved ones, the region's communication infrastructure is well-equipped to meet your needs.

CONCLUSION

Your journey through the Amalfi Coast, as outlined in this guide, promises to be a memorable adventure filled with breathtaking views, rich cultural experiences, and countless opportunities for relaxation and exploration. From the rugged beauty of the coastline to the charming historic towns, the Amalfi Coast offers a unique blend of natural wonders and human craftsmanship that is sure to leave a lasting impression.

As you navigate through the winding streets of Positano, soak up the history of Amalfi, and take in the panoramic views from Ravello, remember that every corner of this region has its own story to tell. The vibrant markets, exquisite cuisine, and warm hospitality of the locals all contribute to the unique charm that makes the Amalfi Coast a world-renowned destination.

While planning your trip, it's important to consider the practical aspects such as transportation, accommodation, and local customs. This guide has provided detailed information on how to get around, where to stay, and what to expect, ensuring that you are well-prepared for every aspect of your visit. Whether you are traveling alone, with a partner, or with family, the Amalfi Coast caters to a wide range of interests and needs, making it an ideal destination for all types of travelers.

Health and safety are paramount when traveling, and this guide has included essential information on medical services, emergency contacts, and general safety tips. By familiarizing yourself with these details, you can ensure a smooth and worry-free journey, allowing you to focus on enjoying the beauty and culture of the region.

Communication is key to making the most of your trip, and the guide has covered various options for staying connected, from mobile data plans to local Wi-Fi availability. Keeping in touch with loved ones and accessing important information is made easy with the numerous options available on the Amalfi Coast.

The region's festivals, local customs, and traditional practices offer a glimpse into the vibrant cultural heritage of the Amalfi Coast. Participating in these events and respecting local traditions will enrich your experience and create lasting memories. Whether it's enjoying a local festival, visiting artisan shops, or savoring traditional cuisine, embracing the local culture will deepen your connection to this enchanting region.

As you prepare for your journey, consider the environmental impact of your travels. The Amalfi Coast is a fragile ecosystem, and responsible tourism practices are essential to preserving its natural beauty for future generations. Simple actions such as reducing waste, respecting wildlife, and supporting local businesses can make a significant difference.

The Amalfi Coast is a destination that captivates the heart and soul of every traveler. Its stunning landscapes, historic landmarks, and welcoming communities create a perfect blend of relaxation and adventure. This travel guide has equipped you with the knowledge and resources needed to make the most of your visit, ensuring that you experience all the wonders this region has to offer.

As you set out on your journey, keep an open mind and a curious spirit. Allow yourself to be immersed in the sights, sounds, and flavors of the Amalfi Coast. Each moment spent exploring this magical region will contribute to an unforgettable adventure that you will cherish for years to come.

Made in the USA
Las Vegas, NV
15 December 2024